WATER

The Earth series traces the historical significance and cultural history of natural phenomena. Written by experts who are passionate about their subject, titles in the series bring together science, art, literature, mythology, religion and popular culture, exploring and explaining the planet we inhabit in new and exciting ways.

Series editor: Daniel Allen

In the same series
Air Peter Adey
Cave Ralph Crane and Lisa Fletcher
Desert Roslynn D. Haynes
Earthquake Andrew Robinson
Fire Stephen J. Pyne
Flood John Withington
Islands Stephen A. Royle
Moon Edgar Williams
Tsunami Richard Hamblyn
Volcano James Hamilton
Water Veronica Strang
Waterfall Brian J. Hudson

Water

Veronica Strang

REAKTION BOOKS

For my sister Helen, who never forgets that blood is thicker than water.

Published by
Reaktion Books Ltd
33 Great Sutton Street
London EC1V 0DX, UK
www.reaktionbooks.co.uk

First published 2015

Printed and bound in China by 1010 Printing International Ltd

A catalogue record for this book is available from the British Library

ISBN 978 1 78023 432 8

CONTENTS

Introduction

Pause for a moment and turn inward. Perhaps you are curled up comfortably on a sofa, maybe sitting on a train as it roars under a city or squashed into a seat on a bus or aeroplane. But wherever you are, water – that unique fluid composed of hydrogen and oxygen – is flowing through you: carrying your blood through veins and arteries; hydrating your flesh and bone; conducting the electrical charges that allow thoughts to fizz through your brain; cleansing waste products; softening your skin; washing over the corneas of your eyes as you read. Without a constant flow of water to keep all of these complex systems functioning, your body would move rapidly through stress, to pain, and then to complete breakdown.

But, though we can enjoy the refreshment of a cool drink, hear the pulse of fluids through our internal systems, even feel the relief of releasing a full bladder, the hydrology of our physical selves flows mostly at a subterranean level, beneath our everyday consciousness. Still we are aware that these vital undercurrents are there, in the same way that we know that they are going on all around us, in the houseplants or gardens that we water (or allow to wither), in the crops we grow, in the animals we live with, in the ecosystems we inhabit, and in the weather that sends rain to drum against the windows and gush down rivers and streams.

The flow of water through every organism on Earth is not just physical. Water also permeates our emotions and imaginations, providing metaphors to think with. It flows through religious beliefs as well as political, economic and social practices. It is literally essential to every aspect of life, and it always has been. So this book is about human relationships with water: how we experience it; what we believe and understand about it; how we use it both literally and imaginatively. Through myriad cultural lenses, humans have worshipped, loved and feared water, have been connected by it and have fought over it. Today, as conflicts over freshwater resources intensify, and even the great oceans are feeling the pressures of climate change and pollution, our bio-cultural relationship with water remains central not only to human well-being, but to that of every living species.

What does 'bio-cultural' mean? In many parts of the indus-trialized world it has become commonplace to talk about 'Nature' and 'Culture' as if these were separate domains. But what we think of as 'Nature' is seen, understood and experienced through a cultural lens. And 'Culture' is located in and affected by the material properties of the world we inhabit. Human conscious-ness resides in bio-cultural bodies, with their own physiological, Porto, Portugal.

chemical and genetic realities, which affect and are affected by cultural ideas and practices. How humans engage with water is therefore as cultural as it is natural and, over time and space, the ways that societies have thought about, understood and acted upon water are in some ways fantastically diverse, and in others remarkably consistent.[1]

Because water flows through every aspect of our lives and appears in myriad forms in every part of the world, there are vast and complex oceans of information on this topic. There is no way to distil these here; what we have, more realistically, is an account that skips across the story like a pebble, landing only fleetingly on its surface. But, hopefully, in doing so it touches upon the key things, and provides a sense of how human lives have connected with water over time.

1 Water on Earth

Water in space

Few things express the interaction between humankind and the material world as comprehensively as water. Its particular characteristics are central to the way that all biological organisms have evolved over time, and simultaneously central to how each human society experiences water, and thinks about what it is and what it means. Many societies, observing water's life-generating processes, have concluded that all life on Earth must have come from water, and this explanation has formed the basis of many 'origin myths' over time. But how did water and life come to Earth in the first place?

There are various forms of (or ingredients for) water in space. The solar system itself is believed to have begun 4.5 billion years ago as a spiral of gas composed mostly of hydrogen. Recently, astronomers spotted a vast cloud of water vapour floating around a black hole 10 billion light years away, estimating that it holds 140 trillion times the mass of water in the earth's oceans. Several celestial bodies appear to have hydrospheres of some kind, and the Jovian moons Ganymede and Europa are thought to have deep oceans, albeit under thick layers of ice.

In 1876 an Italian priest, Pietro Secchi, spotted what appeared to be channels (*canali*) on Mars. The map of these produced in 1877 by astronomer Giovanni Schiaparelli, and the translation of *canali* into English as 'canals', sparked a belief amongst some fellow stargazers, such as American astronomer Percival Lowell, that these must have been constructed by an

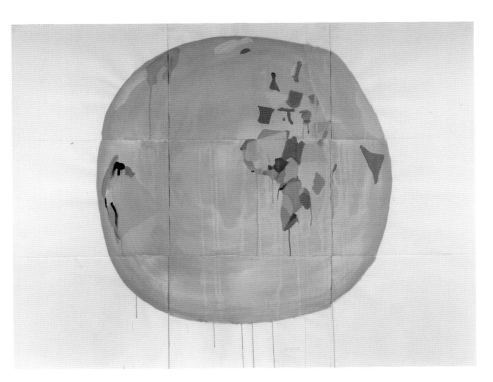

Ruth Barabash,
Planète, 2002,
gouache on paper.

intelligent civilization.[1] This enticing notion persisted until clearer photographs were taken during the space explorations of the 1960s and '70s, and it is now thought that most of the water on the Red Planet is locked in a cryosphere of ice and permafrost.

So why did Earth become a blue planet, characterized by vast ocean expanses and landscapes scribbled with the tracery of massive river systems? How did it gain a hydrosphere that could generate multifarious forms of life? At the same time that astronomers were getting excited about *canali*-building Martians, Svante Arrhenius suggested that living particles had either arrived on Earth via 'radiopanspermia', travelling along light beams from space, or that microbes or spores had been carried here clinging to meteorites. Until recently it was believed that water had arrived with the frequent showers of meteorites that fell to Earth in its formative stages, but according to astrophysicist Martin Ward:

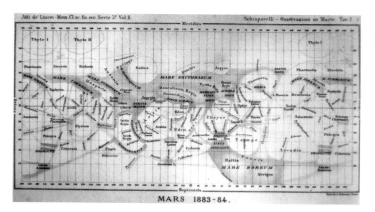

Map of *canali* on Mars by Giovanni Schiaparelli, 1888.

Recent observations suggest the isotopic ratios of water, i.e. H_2O versus D_2O (deuterium is an isotope of hydrogen), are not the same in comets as [in water] found on Earth. It is now thought that asteroids may contain significant amounts of water, and that impacts of these during the so-called 'Late Heavy Bombardment' about 4 billion years ago, may have been the source of much of the Earth's water.[2]

Even today, there is no scientific consensus about the origin of water on Earth.[3] However, the ideas initiated by Charles Darwin and Louis Pasteur offer a compelling vision of chemical evolution, in which sunlight and radioactivity provided sufficient heat and energy for the creation of water, and a feisty interaction of amino acids, carbon monoxide, carbon dioxide, nitrogen and other organic matter enabled the emergence of living cells with their own metabolic and reproductive processes.

The properties of water

When, about 2 billion years ago, photosynthesis created an atmosphere containing oxygen, multicellular organisms were able to develop, and off the earth's biota (flora and fauna) went: through the curlicue shells of Cambrian ocean fossils, through toothsome Jurassic beasts, all the way to bipedal naked apes able to imagine Martian canals. But the oldest cells found on the blue planet originated deep in its oceans. Life on Earth has been aquatic for most of its history, simmering in the depths for nearly 4 billion years and only making it onto land about 450 million years ago. In this sense, the multiple cultural and historical explanations echoing the notion that 'water is life', or that 'all life comes from water' are right, albeit challenged in their universality by research on other worlds.[4] As Philip Ball notes,

> recent confirmation that there is at least one world rich in organic molecules on which rivers and perhaps seas are filled with nonaqueous fluid – the liquid hydrocarbons of Titan – might now bring some focus or even urgency to the question as to whether water is indeed a unique and universal matrix of life, or just the one that exists on our planet.[5]

An asteroid prior to impact.

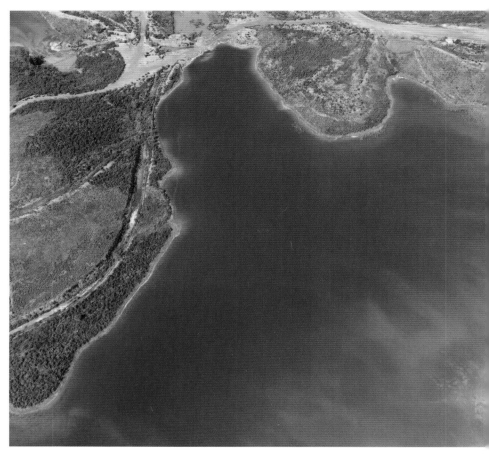

However, on Earth at least, multicellular organisms do indeed depend upon the particular properties of water. So what are these? Well, above all, water connects: its molecules are more negatively charged at one end, and more positively charged at the other, which means that it is able not only to bond with itself, but to form complex molecules with a vast range of other substances. But – as with all of water's material properties – this process can be reversed: water can also 'dissociate', letting go of the substances with which it has bonded. Its ability to separate and recombine makes it a 'universal solvent', able to carry other chemicals, for example oxygen and nutrients, through

Oxidized iron minerals in water, Rio Tinto (Red River), Huelva Province, Spain.

living organisms such as ourselves, and to leave them there. This characteristic also means, of course, that it can be readily contaminated, bringing in harmful rather than helpful substances. But another major advantage of this bonding capacity is that water can and does pick up wastes and toxins, carrying them out of organisms and their internal hydrological systems.

Water's characteristics as a solvent were central to evolutionary progress: it dissolved a lot of the simple organic compounds in the earth's early atmosphere and helped to form more complex mixes. The first living cells – those able to replicate – formed as microscopic aquatic plants (phytoplankton) energized by the sun as they drifted through the oceans. And when multicellular organisms evolved, they did so with fluid internal systems in which water enabled the absorption of nutrients and the expulsion of wastes. Blood contains more dissolved fluids than any other substance, which led Johann Wolfgang von Goethe (1749–1832) to describe it as the most complicated compound fluid on Earth.[6] Water's connective abilities are also critical in enabling electrochemical transmission. As well as carrying blood and other vital chemicals to the brain, water supports the electrical

The Rhône Glacier
in the 19th century.

potential of brain neurons, and is therefore quite literally 'a stream of consciousness'.

Water's molecular composition is also integral to one of its most recognizable material properties: the capacity to undergo physical transformations in form, from ice to fluid and from fluid to steam. These pertain at every micro and macro level: the transformations that take place at a domestic level, between kettle, fridge and freezer, are mirrored on a planetary scale as water melts from glaciers, flows across landscapes and rises into the clouds. As well as being able to change form reversibly, water is in constant motion: it flows, zigzagging down slopes (again because of its molecular structure) and forming whirlpools in streams. It surges with waves and ripples in the wind. It evaporates elusively into thin air. Bodies of water, transparent and opaque, flicker with light. Thus water is characterized by movement and transformation.

Water also has more subtle, creeping forms of travel: its molecular structure enables capillary action, so that it soaks, permeates and moves through other things. Rising groundwaters keep the earth's soils moist and productive, enabling plants to draw nutrients into their internal systems of fluid transport. Here too lies another major contribution that water makes to sustaining life: through evaporation and transpiration, and through its ability to humidify, it maintains the fluid balance of all living things. And, on a larger scale, its specific heat,[7] and the vast ocean currents,

The Fertilization of Egypt, print by William Blake after Henry Fuseli, to Erasmus Darwin's poem *The Botanic Garden* (1791), showing the ancient Egyptian God Anubis praying to the star Sirius for rain.

Maria Sibylla Merian, *Sea Purslane and Surinam Toad*, c. 1701–5.

Whangarei Falls,
a 26.3-m-high waterfall
in New Zealand.

stabilize the temperatures of seas that would otherwise be far more extreme in their variations, and much less kind to the myriad species that they support.

Water balance is equally critical to the earth's atmosphere, and to the creation of humidity, precipitation and so forth. As Michael Allaby says, 'Weather consists mainly of water in one or another of its forms.'[8] In essence, responding to temperature and pressure, water shape-shifts its way around the planet, appearing here as snow, there as torrential rain and, for at least part of the year, shying away from hot equatorial latitudes.

Rerum AQVA principium, chaos, et fons est, et origo,
Frugibus vnde vigor seminibusque venit.
Adrian. Collaert inuent. sculp. et exud.

Squamigeros homini pisces alimenta ministrat;
Et quo nauagys transeat, aptat iter.
Corn. Kil. Dussl.

Along with temperature, the coming of the rain, or not, and the speed at which this arrives, is one of the most critical issues for all organic species.

Adriaen Collaert, *The Four Elements: Aqua, c.* 1580.

So the question about where water comes from has long exercised the human imagination. Ancient societies believed that beneficent deities either sent the rain to assist their endeavours, or withheld it (or sent punitive amounts) when people misbehaved. And many recognized some kind of relationship between the sun and water, often defining these as major collaborative deities.

There were also early secular efforts to analyse the world in material terms. The Chinese defined five elements – earth, water, fire, wood and metal – and the Greeks identified four: earth, air, water and fire. The Greeks were also interested in *archē*, the notion of a primary substance. Heraclitus, who famously described the inexorable nature of time by saying that 'you cannot step into the same river twice', thought that fire was the primary element from which all things arose. Others thought that *archē* was composed of water and fire. Thales of Miletus, the 'Father of Science', proposed the cosmological thesis (later drawn on by Aristotle) that the world emerged from water.

In thinking about where water came from, springs seemed to provide a useful clue, leading early scholars to suggest that water rose from a vast subterranean reservoir, which Aristotle called Tartarus. Plato agreed, envisaging vast underground caverns, and this notion that rivers and streams came from deep within the earth persisted until the eighteenth century.

But there was also irrefutable evidence of water falling from above and, without concepts of atmospheres or hydrospheres,

Athanasius Kircher,
illustration from
Mundus Subterraneus
(c. 1664).

many societies envisaged rivers in the sky as well as below the earth's surface. The ancient Greeks imagined the earth surrounded by a whirling stream of water, which they named Okeanus, its nomenclature suggesting an upper world that mirrored the land and waterscapes below. The Milky Way features in a range of cosmological explanations as a river: the early Egyptians thought that the Nile had two entities, one earthbound, 'the other, the celestial Nile which flows across the heavens and can be seen as a luminous river'.[9] The

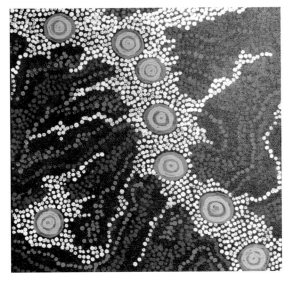

Seven Sisters (Milky Way) Dreaming, 2009, by Aboriginal artist Gabriella Possum Nungurrayi, acrylic on linen.

ancient Chinese called it Tiān Hé, the Heavenly River, or Yin He, the Silvery Way; Akkadians described it as the River of the Abyss; and Indians as the Bed of the Ganges.[10] Mesolithic hunter-gatherers in the Baltic envisaged a three-tier world – sky, middle (earth) and underworld – linked by a cosmic 'river',[11] and in Australian Aboriginal culture the Milky Way's glittering stars were seen as a serpentine 'sky river' weaving through constellations depicting their totemic beings.

Through various cultural lenses, people also recognized the influence of heavenly bodies on water. Many religious explanations focused on sun and moon deities, and there were diverse ideas about how water actually reached the earth. For example, resonating with ancient Mayan ideas about water and fertility, the Greek Stoics' astral theories proposed that dew descended along the moon's rays to the earth, and had magical powers. This belief led to its collection and use in early alchemy in Europe, a practice that persisted among rural populations into the twentieth century.[12] Hippocrates went so far as to posit a material relationship between water and the sun, suggesting that there were two kinds of water, light and dark, the former being attracted and raised by the sun.[13] His experiments with evaporation were foundational in establishing the idea that the attributes of the physical world could be discovered through experimentation.

Sparked by these early forays into scientific thinking, inquisitive minds continued to puzzle over the elements and their material composition. The Swiss scientist Philippus von Hohenheim, better known as Paracelsus (1493–1541), suggested that air could become water. Prior to the understanding that plants could draw CO_2 from the atmosphere via photosynthesis, a Flemish chemist called Jan Baptist Van Helmont (1579–1644) strengthened this belief by showing that a willow branch given nothing but rainwater could increase its weight from 2.3 to 74.4 kg (5 to 164 lb) over five years, which led him to argue that water and air were the only two key elements and that water could become both organic and inorganic matter.

With the compelling evidence of agriculture at hand, this view held sway for the next century. It took until the 1700s to reach a scientific realization that water is composed of oxygen and hydrogen. There are several contenders as to who reached this conclusion first, but the laurels (at least for publishing most rapidly) generally go to an Englishman – a clergyman, appropriately called Joseph Priestley – who in 1774 described his discovery of a new gas, oxygen. Meanwhile, in Paris, Antoine-Laurent Lavoisier (1743–1794) showed that water could be made by burning an element, which he named hydrogen.[14] A vision of water in molecular form was first provided by the 'founder of atomic theory', John Dalton (1766–1844), a physicist, chemist, meteorologist (and also a Quaker) from the north of England.[15] And, building on this work, Swedish chemist Jöns Jakob Berzelius (1779–1848) proved that the ratio of hydrogen to oxygen in water molecules is 2:1, thus defining water as H_2O or HOH.

During the same period, scientists such as Swedish astronomer Anders Celsius (1701–1744) and Martin Strömer (1707–1770) examined the properties of water, defining its freezing and boiling points.[16] German inventor Daniel Gabriel Fahrenheit (1686–1736), who came up with his own scale,

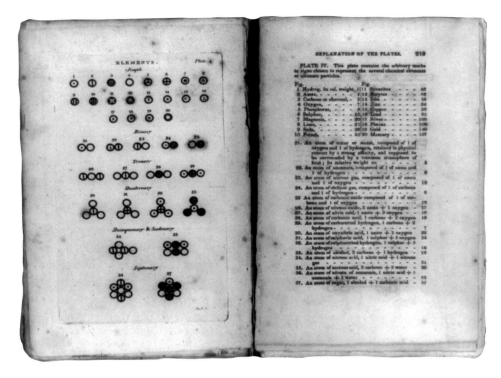

found that the latter differed with variations in air pressure. Thus, high in the Andes, where water reaches boiling point at a lower temperature, it can take a very long time to boil an egg.

Table showing various chemical elements and their atomic weights, from John Dalton's *A New System of Chemical Philosophy* (1808–27).

Moving water

As well as deconstructing water as an element, scientists continued to wrestle with questions about how it made its way around the world. The central narrative of modern hydrology is the overturning of the 'subterranean' hypothesis, and the establishment of a vision of a hydrologic cycle. The pre-Christian Roman architect and engineer Vitruvius provided an important piece of the puzzle with the recognition that underground water sources were replenished by rainfall and snow melt. But the first coherently cyclical scientific vision came from Leonardo da Vinci (1452–1519), who described water as the driving force of all Nature and provided a clear understanding that the water pouring through the world's river systems did so repeatedly.[17]

That is not to say that earlier human societies had never thought about water movements in cyclical, seasonal terms. For example Australian Aboriginal concepts of the 'Rainbow' or 'Rainbow Serpent' provide a clear vision of water circling over and under the earth in conjunction with the generation of life from a sacred landscape, and this broader idea is closely tied to detailed local understandings of rainfall patterns and water movements across and under the land.[18]

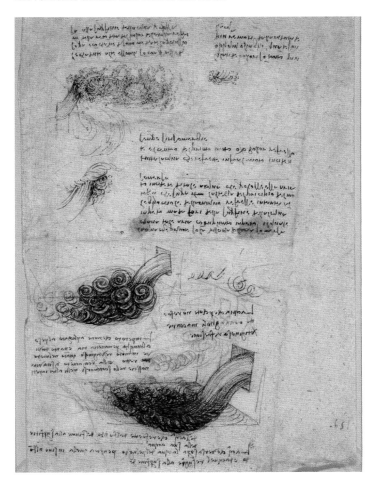

Studies of flowing water by Leonardo da Vinci, from the *Codex Leicester*, 1506–13.

However, though they might also be said to rely on long-term observations of empirical evidence, localized ethno-science and hydrotheological explanations of this kind have tended not to make it into mainstream 'scientific' narratives such as 'hydrology' which, though they emerged from particular geographic regions, have taken centre stage at a global level. These more dominant discourses focus on experimentation and 'proof', for example recounting how, in the seventeenth century, Edme Mariotte and Pierre Perrault analysed rainfall and river flow in the Seine watershed, and Edmund Halley calculated that evaporation from the Mediterranean matched the surface run-off in the area.[19]

Even these scientific findings remained tied to religious cosmologies for some time. Jamie Linton highlights an important relationship between Christian theological beliefs of the seventeenth and eighteenth centuries, in which God was assumed to have a grand design, and emerging scientific ideas in which scholars tried to get to grips with hydrological processes.[20] Under an assumption that God was in charge, Christian 'natural theology' favoured a vision in which water's movements were seen as being reliably controlled, with rainfall arriving regularly and in manageable quantities (unless – with an echo of earlier belief systems – humans transgressed God's laws and required punishment).

The Qur'an and the Bible share similar narratives about rainfall as the product of monotheistic beneficence, and there was considerable intellectual leadership in early hydrology in ancient Egypt and contiguous areas. Over time, however, perspectives from arid regions were subsumed by ideas emerging in more temperate northern climes about God's reliable provision of water, and these formed the central motif in emergent ideas about the hydrologic cycle. As appreciation grew of the material processes through which water moved through the world, hydrological explanations resulted in a new hybrid concept, which Yi-Fu Tuan describes as the 'hydrotheological cycle'.[21]

With increasing divergence between 'rational' science and faith in the nineteenth and twentieth centuries, beliefs in a beneficent guiding deity segued into secular visions of a hydrological

Steam rising from a hot spring at Wai-O-Tapu, New Zealand.

process under the direction of Nature. Thus Walter Langbein and William Hoyt describe the water cycle as 'one of nature's grand plans', a seemingly inevitable 'engine' of water movement.[22]

The hydrologic cycle is the most fundamental principle of hydrology. Water evaporates from the oceans and the land surface, is carried over the Earth in atmospheric circulation as water vapor, precipitates again as rain or snow, is intercepted by trees and vegetation, provides runoff on the land surface, infiltrates into soils, recharges groundwater, discharges into streams, and ultimately, flows out into the oceans from which it will eventually evaporate once again.

This immense water engine, fuelled by solar energy, driven by gravity, proceeds endlessly in the presence or absence of human activity.[23]

So, just as Christian natural theology, with its vision of a grand design, had led to a negative view of drier geographic regions, a vision of arid places as hydrologically dysfunctional was reinforced by experiments conducted primarily in moderate temperate climes. Both envisaged a reliable water cycle and assumed – with major implications for developments in water use and management – that something must be morally 'wrong' (and must be put right) in drier geographic areas, or in those with more variable patterns of rainfall. In reality, human societies inhabit highly diverse hydrological environments; they have either adapted successfully to locally specific conditions or, trying to conform to an idealized hydrological vision, have overridden these with increasingly directive technologies and commensurately extreme ecological impacts.

Water limits

Water, water every where, /Nor any drop to drink.[24]

Earth may be the blue planet, but 93.3 per cent of its water lies in its oceans and has varying levels of salinity. Fresh water is either found in rivers and lakes, contained in aquifers and underground basins, or held in ice. The largest reserve of fresh water on the planet is in the glaciers found in the high mountains of every continent except Australia. About a third of the world's human populations, and a considerable percentage of its plant and animal species, depend on these for seasonal meltwater, thus the shrinkage of the glaciers due to climate change has significant hydrological implications. The retreat of the glaciers is happening fast. Thirty years ago, many could be seen and heard crunching and munching their way across lower mountain valleys. Now, just a few decades on, they have literally melted away into the higher reaches of the mountains.

The water stored under the earth's surface lies at various levels, and the point at which soil pores or rock voids are completely saturated constitutes the 'water table'. Groundwaters are 'recharged' seasonally, with glacial and snow meltwater and rainfall, but they are also composed largely of fossil reserves accumulated through advancing and retreating ice ages, over the whole of geological time. Thus overabstraction (taking more water than arrives in annual recharge) means that their levels, and thus the water table, are falling in many parts of the world, sometimes descending out of reach. This abstraction – because most precipitation falls back into the larger areas represented by the oceans – also composes a quarter of the increase in sea levels occurring annually.

The oceans, as Aristotle rightly hypothesized, provide much of the 'sweet' fresh water that is drawn upwards to fall as rain. If we think of it in terms of sheer volume, Poul Astrup and his

Bethells Beach, North Island, New Zealand.

Glacier at Mount Cook,
New Zealand.

colleagues estimated that the yearly net evaporation into the earth's atmosphere comprises about 430,000 km³ from oceans, and 70,000 km³ from continents. Because mountains capture clouds and rain, however, the land masses get about 110,000 km³ in rainfall, so making a net gain of about 40,000 km³ each year.[25] But of course this is distributed far from evenly around the globe.

In this sense, the earth's planetary fluid system is not unlike that of its multifarious organic life forms. It contains some parts with less water content than others, but even in these, water is vital to the successful maintenance of life: all biota depend on the movement of water through air, soil and cells, and all are connected by water. This sense of connection is nicely captured by Vladimir Vernadsky's ideas.[26] In the 1920s, Vernadsky was inspired by early Greek debates about the 'nature' of the earth and its waters, and by Johannes Kepler (1571–1630), a German mathematician and astronomer who – long before James Lovelock resuscitated the Greek notion of *Gaia* – described the earth as a living being composed of sentient, interactive particles.[27]

Vernadsky highlighted the point that not only had all life forms emerged from the oceans to populate *terra firma*, they remained materially connected by the flow of water between them. This vision of a living, interconnected biosphere was picked up by scholars such as Lynn Margulis and Dianna and Mark McMenamin to describe the 'symbiogenesis' of all flora and fauna, comprising, as the McMenamins put it, a 'hyper-sea' of biota connected by water, in which humankind, rather than flinging out its chest and straddling the earth like a Colossus, is presented more modestly, as one of the myriad species participating in a larger flow of organic life.[28]

2 Living Water

The sea inside

One of the reasons that it is easy to envision a connective 'hypersea' of water linking all living things is that water behaves in similar ways at every scale. In a microcosmic echo of planetary circulations, water flows through even the smallest organisms in what we could call 'hyposeas', connecting each part of them. Thus in the human body, as in larger systems, water mediates interactions between all of the different materials and processes involved in maintaining life. And, as in the wider environment, the variability of these materials depends both on their molecular structure and on their water content. Even now, millions of evolutionary years after biota emerged from the oceans, human bodies are approximately 67 per cent water.[1] Human teeth are like rocks, having just over 12 per cent. Bones, which in metaphor serve as the body's timber, are 22 per cent water. Brain tissue, like a fertile, resource-rich wetland, is about 73 per cent, and blood – though certainly thicker than water – is 80 to 92 per cent H_2O.

About two-thirds of the water in human bodies is 'intracellular' – inside our cells. The other third is comprised of 'extracellular' fluids such as blood plasma, and 'transcellular' fluids, which surround the cells, carry nutrition and oxygen to them and remove metabolic wastes. Water's properties as a universal solvent are central to all of these complex chemical processes. It aids digestion, transforming sucrose via hydrolysis into glucose and fructose, which can be utilized by body cells. It keeps mucous

Muriwai Beach,
New Zealand.

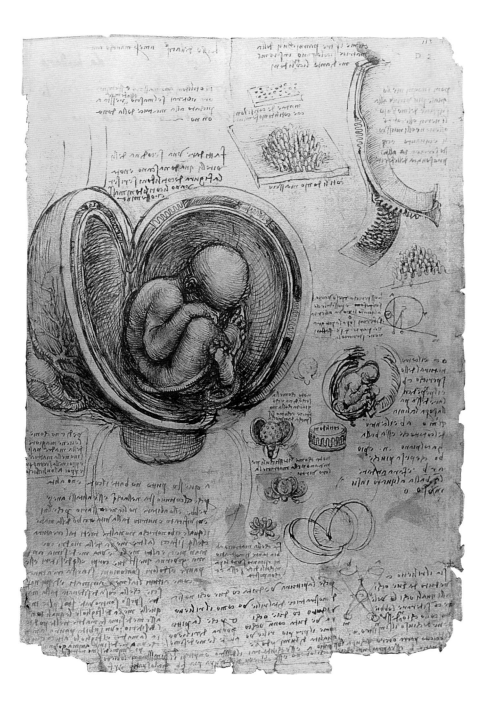

membranes moist, regulates temperature, lubricates joints, moisturizes the skin and serves as a shock absorber inside the eyes, the spine and of course the womb.

As most of us learned in school biology lessons, water flows through the body in two hydraulic systems: through an active blood circulatory system provided by the heart muscles (blood is pumped from the heart into arteries, then to capillaries, and returns to the heart through veins), and a more passive lymphatic system reliant upon body movements. Constant hydration is crucial: human bodies cannot store much water, losing two to three litres a day – about half through excretion and the other half by breathing and sweating. Much of this hydration comes from food, in particular fruit and many vegetables which, at about 90 per cent, have the highest water content of any food substances.

Deprived of water, people and animals die within a few days, though some will hang on – in increasing misery – for several weeks. Drinking water excessively (as occurs with some mental illnesses) can also be physically disastrous, leading to critical dilutions of sodium levels (hyponatremia) and overloads to cells. Water intoxication produces the same effects as drowning in fresh water: fluids can enter the lungs; pressure on the brain and nerves produces behaviours resembling those caused by alcohol; swelling of the brain tissues can cause seizures, coma and ultimately death.

Maintaining a water balance is equally important for all organic species. Plants, many of which are composed of high percentages of water, share with animals a dependence upon fluid transport processes. They wither rapidly without water, and will similarly experience cellular breakdown if overloaded with it. Ecosystems, whether local, regional or planetary in scale, function according to similar principles, requiring a particular hydraulic balance – the right amount of water, at the right pace, and at the right time. So, at all levels, water's life-giving potential relies not only on its properties, but also on a carefully balanced flow in its movements.

Of course these are the explanations of a globalized scientific model. Specific cultural explanations of hydrological

The phases of the foetus's development in the womb, notebook sketch by Leonardo da Vinci, *c.* 1510–13.

systems also make intellectual leaps between micro and macro processes. For example, the Qollahuaya people in the Andes draw topographical and physiological hydraulic systems together, seeking inspiration for understanding human bodily processes from their sacred mountains (*allyu*) and their waterways.[2] The body is therefore seen analogously as having a vertical axis with ducts through which blood and water (as well as air and fat) flow inward, centripetally, to the heart (*sonco*) and then centrifugally from the heart to the limbs. Thus the *sonco* is an internal aquifer in which all functions – respiratory, digestive and reproductive – are combined, and from which secondary fluids (bile, faeces, milk, semen, sweat and urine) must be eliminated.

Understanding of physiological and ecological processes, and their needs for hydraulic balance, is readily extended to thinking about how water flows through other material systems. Domestic spaces, whether at the scale of an individual home or as part of extended urban infrastructures, need water supplies piped in and sewage piped out. Whether in a garden vegetable patch or in vast fields of commercial wheat, the supply of water in the right amounts and at the right time is vital to food production. Industries, too, need water at multiple stages of their

Bas-relief of Bireme Roman warships, probably liburnians, from 'The Reliefs of Trajan's Column' by Conrad Cichorius, 113 CE.

manufacturing processes and for many centuries societies have transported their material products to each other via waterways and across oceans.

Water out of place

Mary Douglas famously cited Lord Chesterfield's comment that dirt is simply 'matter out of place' and so indicative of the disordering of an orderly system.[3] Just as all of the world's material and social processes require an orderly flow of water, all can be disordered or disrupted by impediments to flow, or by too much flow – at which point water ceases to be life-giving sustenance and becomes an invasive tide. Water can also be a major medium for carrying 'matter out of place'. Its capacity to bond with pollutants at a molecular level (for example in carrying toxins into the bloodstream) is echoed in its ability to carry pollution across larger material boundaries: slurry into waterways; foul flooding into domestic spaces.

All of the systems dependent upon the flow of water have some mechanisms for cleansing themselves, relying equally on water's abilities to dilute or carry polluting wastes away. Thus bodies and plants eliminate unwanted substances through emissions and transpirations. Water treatment companies remove sewage from waste water and then rely on the environment to

Waste water
treatment in a
Wessex sewage plant.

finish the job in what they call the 'magic mile': the distance it is commonly believed to take for a river to disperse remaining pollutants sufficiently, or absorb them via aquatic plants and microorganisms. At sea, marine organisms gobble and (eventually) break down oil spills. And in this way the functional 'order' of each system is – theoretically – restored.

As this implies, in the cyclical movements of water through micro and macro systems, there is a delicate balance between creativity and entropy. Contemporary physics posits that isolated systems tend to degenerate from order to disorder. So it is both the ability of each system to maintain order and, critically, the flow of connections between systems, that constitute their sustainability. There has been some experimentation with contained systems. For example, water recycling on NASA spaceships in the future will reuse almost every molecule of water produced by their inhabitants – humans and rats alike. Their urine, and even the humidity produced by their breath and sweat, will be recycled by each station's Environmental Control and Life Support System. Drinking rat urine (or rat breath for that matter) may seem unappealing but, as NASA's water processing specialist Layne Carter put it, 'It might sound disgusting, but water leaving the space station's purification machines will be cleaner than what most of us drink on Earth.'[4]

Still, without interconnection to other systems, nothing can be sustained indefinitely. All of the multiple water flows on Earth rely ultimately on connections with its largest recycling system – its hydrosphere – and it is the overreaching of the capacities of this system to absorb pollution and maintain order that is now producing climate change and raising the spectre of potential entropic chaos on a planetary scale.

Back to the future

> In the beginning there was nothing but water, water, water.
>
> Indian tribal song[5]

Chaos, of course, is where it all began. The science of the earth's origins suggests that the orderly circulation of water through its multiple organic systems emerged from material chaos. We can thank the ancient Greeks for this term, *khaos*, which (without knowing just how accurate this was in a solar system founded in a cloud of hydrogen) was redeployed by Val Helmont to describe 'gas'. The Greeks had used it more broadly, to talk about formless pre-matter – the space between the heavens and the earth. And it is this idea of things 'taking form' out of formlessness which defines the relationship between order and chaos: a relationship that is always fluid, and always, quite literally, a matter of life and death. As the idea of 'resources' so readily

The International Space Station (ISS).

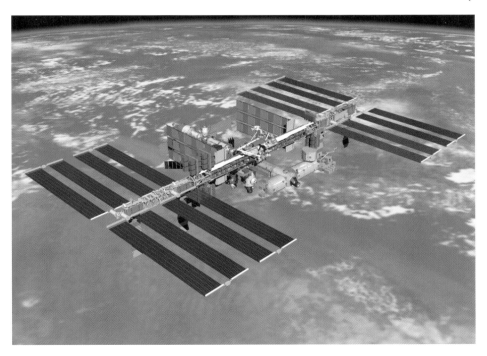

expresses, water (as well as other material things) can be seen as potential – and in this sense, water is a kind of über potential, enabling all other material events. But the potentiality of water is dynamic: organic things, creatures and persons may take form, but as fluid 'works in progress' they don't get to keep it.

Being blessed and/or cursed (depending on your view) with a consciousness of mortality, human societies have known this all along. From the earliest stages of storytelling, their narratives have described flows of being through time, using observations of the movements of water through the world to articulate ideas about taking form as humans, and returning to formless-ness upon death. Micro-level views of human life cycles have been projected onto the cosmos through culturally diverse origin myths in which the world 'takes form' from nothingness and all living creatures emerge from creative primal waters. In these stories of whirling *khaos*, of vast creative oceans and life-making storms, water is, in the true sense of the word, primordial, the chaos before order, the oblivion into which order can always dissolve. For example, if we return to the Australian Aboriginal hydrotheological cycle and its powerful, generative Rainbow Serpent, we find Dreamtime stories that tell how ancestral beings rose up or spewed out of this water being, from the wild and dangerous waters under the land, to make all the features of the landscape. Then they sank back down, remaining in the land as a hidden pool of ancestral power. This pool is also the source of the human spirit-beings that 'jump up' from the ancestral waters to materialize or 'become visible' in human form. At the end of each individual life cycle, they return to their watery home to be reunited with their ancestors, 'becom-ing invisible' and so dissolving back into collective formless potential.[6]

Like the Australian Rainbow Serpent, creative water deities in many religions have taken serpentine form, echoing the shape of the water of which they were conceptually composed. In New Zealand, the Maori describe how a water god, Tangaroa, formed the world out of an era of creative chaos (*te kore*).[7] Throughout the Americas powerful water beings – the Hopi Water Serpent,

Aztec double-headed
serpent ornament,
c. 15th–16th century,
turquoise mosaic
wood carving.

Paluukong, the Pueblo horned serpent, Awanyu, and the Aztec plumed serpent, Quetzalcóatl – acted as primal creative forces.[8]

Many religions have incorporated into their cosmological explanations not only broad ideas about water's creative potential, but also more immediate understandings of procreation.[9] This is reflected in their ideas about the deities that embody the world's life-making processes. Edward Shafer reminds us that such matter is typically composed of both female and male principles, or androgynous combinations of the two,[10] working in complementary creative union:

> Sexual ambiguity is characteristic of the rain spirits of various cultures. Among the African Bushmen, for instance, the destructive thunderheads that breed lightning and hail are masculine, while the soft clouds that shed fertilizing, misty rain are feminine . . . In the earliest literature of China . . . the colored bow in the sky is an attribute or a manifestation of a beautiful rain goddess. Nevertheless,

there appears to have been a linguistic distinction between male and female rainbows in early China. Some evidence indicates that *ghung* was the male and *ngei* was the female. Occasionally both were displayed in the sky together.[11]

These ideas flow across human history. *Enuma elish*, the Babylonian creation poem also has female and male elements, Ti'amat, 'the salt water abyss', and Apsu, 'the sweet water abyss'. It describes how the mingling of these primordial waters enabled the creation of the world and the birth of the gods.[12] Bronze Age clay tablets recounting Canaanite creation myths centre on the primeval seas of Yam and a storm god, Baal. The Sumerians described Zu, a serpent of water and chaos, and in the Egyptian Pyramid Texts 'The Creator-Primeval Serpent' of Egyptian mythology declares that he is 'the overflow of the Primeval Flood . . . He who emerged from the waters'.[13]

Historical shifts from early Nature religions to more humanized deities tended to bring with them a vision of God taking control of the primordial waters. Thus the Qur'an states that God made water the basis of creation, and placed his throne upon it.[14] The twelfth-century writer al-Kisa'l, in the *Tales of the Prophets* (*Qisas al-anbiya*), says, 'Then the water was told, "Be still". And, it was still, awaiting God's command. This is limpid water, which contains neither impurity nor foam.'[15]

Drawing from Mesopotamian and Canaanite myths, the ancient Hebrews similarly described the universe as beginning in a state of formlessness. In the Bible, as in the Qur'an, it is God who brings order into the chaos of Genesis, giving form to things, and calming chaotic seas into purposeful flows.

The Earth was without form and void, and darkness was upon the face of the deep; and the wind of God was hovering over the face of the waters.

And God said, 'Let there be a firmament in the midst of the waters . . . Let the waters under the heavens be gathered together in one place, and let the dry land appear.' And it was so.

God called the dry land Earth, and the waters that
were gathered together he called Seas. And God saw that
it was good.[16]

However, creating order from chaos was by no means
straightforward. Many origin myths describe epic battles to
subdue the primordial seas. Aboriginal stories, Sumerian and
Babylonian myths, as well as those of the Old Testament, all
relate tales of vast floods: a deluge which represented a return
to disorder and chaos.[17] The restoration of order depended on
ancestral heroes and gods powerful enough to take control. In
Northern Australia, Aboriginal song cycles recall how the Two
Brothers chopped down trees and created mountains to hold the
sea back; the Babylonian God/hero Marduk conquered Ti'amat.
And Yahweh gained authority over Leviathan, and handed him
to Job as a 'perpetual slave'.

When the waters saw you, O God,
When the waters saw you, they were afraid,
Yea, the deep trembled.[18]

Yet that image, that vision of a return to formless chaos,
remains with humankind as an image of death and dissolution,
disrupting the orderly flow of being and time. In keeping with
its dual nature, water is thus both potential life and death.

Living water

It is from these creative depths that cosmologies around the world
draw ideas about 'living water': the water that flows through
the world enabling life. Whether seen in terms of hydrating
molecules, spiritual power or the pragmatic lifeblood of agricultural production, the notion of living water runs through every
cultural context in some form. It is often expressed through beliefs
in water deities which, like the great leviathans of primal origin,
echo the fluid material properties of water. Though other 'mainstream' religions now dominate, there was a time when almost

Carved *taniwha* on the entrance to a Maori marae, New Zealand.

all societies worshipped water beings of one kind or another, and many such ideas remain, describing the generative and sometimes punitive powers of water. In New Zealand, according to Maori beliefs, rivers are inhabited by *taniwha* and the seas by *marakihau*. The role of these serpentine guardians (*kaitiaki*), like that of the Rainbow serpents on the other side of the Tasman, is to protect local waterways and the groups associated with these.

Snake-like water divinities also appear in the *Mami Wata* religious beliefs that stretch across western, central and southern Africa and into African diasporas elsewhere.[19] Members of such religious groups claim that these beings come from ancient Egyptian *Nommos*.[20] In many versions of Hinduism and Buddhism, water deities called *Nāga*s control rainfall and rivers.[21] In Mexico, thousands gather at Chichen Itza at the spring equinox to watch *Kulkulcan*, the great serpent deity of life and death, descend from the pyramid.

Across China and Japan, dragons and water are inextricably linked: dragon springs gush forth, and cloud dragons drift down from the sky.

In ancient Europe, pathways from Celtic henges led to sacred waterways and, in a practice that continued with the Roman invaders, sacred wells received votive offerings.[22] When

A water feature at Black Dragon Palace, Kunming, China.

A dragon emerging from the clouds. Screen in Kenninji Zen temple, founded in 1202, Kyoto, Japan.

humanized deities and then monotheism subsumed animistic
pagan beliefs, sacred wells were given the names of saints or
(in the Islamic world), prophets, who similarly appropriated
their miraculous healing powers. Thus Zamzam, the sacred well
near the Ka'ba in Mecca, has been the focus of pilgrimages for
millennia, and ninth-century geographer Ibn al-Faqih records
a Hadith (a saying or approved tradition ascribed to the Prophet
Mohammad) that its waters provide 'a remedy for anyone who
suffers'.[23] At an ancient fertility site at Cerne Abbas in Dorset,
a holy well was renamed for St Augustine, and reframed with an
account of how, when he stuck his staff into the ground, water
poured forth.[24]

The font in
Durham Cathedral.

In both the Bible and the Qur'an, a humanized God provides
rain for crops, sending gentle rains to feed the soil:

> We plow the fields and scatter the good seed on the land.
> But it is fed and watered by God's almighty hand.
> He sends us snow in winter, the warmth to swell the grain,
> The breezes and the sunshine, and soft refreshing rain.
> *All good gifts around us*
> *Are sent from Heaven above*
> *Then thank the Lord, thank the Lord for all his love.*[25]

Holy water remained central to Christian and Islamic
religious rituals, most particularly those concerned with key
transitions to and from material being, that is marking birth
(taking form) and death (losing form). Also, resonating with
concepts of pollution and disorder, it is used in rituals concerned
with cleansing sin and, in more extreme cases, with exorcising
demons. The duality of water is maintained even here as, according
to Thomas Csordas, demons can also be carried *into* the body via
polluted water.[26]

As the Church overlapped with the development of secular
ideas, there was a concomitant transition to seeing holy water
more in terms of spiritual enlightenment. Along with the hydro -
theological cycles which attempted to reconcile science and faith,
ideas about *fons sapientiae* represented the attainment of both

wisdom and rationality. More secular ways of thinking, and scientific ideas about the body and material substances, also gave holy wells a new lease of life as healing 'spas'. While holy wells such as Zamzam and Catholic equivalents such as Lourdes continued to rely on religious faith, many such places throughout Europe were transformed into popular health resorts.

Yet there is considerable coherence between these transitions: running through them is a persistent idea concerned with the vitality of 'living water', its powers to cleanse and heal, and a vision of 'health' and 'wealth' (both stemming from the word 'hale' or 'whole'). The etymology here underlines the notion that human health and well-being depend on a 'whole' (moral, intellectual, emotional and physical) system working in an orderly way – not dis-ordered or 'dis-eased'. Such ideas are readily transposed to consider societal and ecological health and 'order', in which living water plays an equally vital role.

Integral to each of these systems, and to the idea of living water, is the necessity of movement. In essence, if water it is not 'quick' it is dead and a vision of stagnation is one of impediment, of being unable to maintain a sufficient flow. 'Living water' therefore encapsulates an understanding that water literally animates material matter and enables life processes.

Phenomenal water

> Whether the weather be fine,
> Or whether the weather be not,
> Whether the weather be cold,
> Or whether the weather be hot,
> We'll weather the weather
> Whatever the weather,
> Whether we like it or not!
> (Anon)

Humans do not merely observe and attach ideas to the multiple movements of water through the world, they also experience them phenomenologically. Simply being in the world means

Health spa fountain,
Czech Republic.

experiencing the weather on an everyday basis and, as noted
earlier, the weather *is* water in motion, water transiting between
forms, water rising and falling, freezing and flowing.[27]

This highlights a reality that human interactions with water
are immediate and often compelling sensory engagements. We feel
the sting of driving rain, or the softer touch of mist. We luxuriate

Fountain in Albert Park, Auckland, New Zealand.

in warm baths and showers; brace ourselves to plunge into colder lakes and seas. We thirst for water in dry climates, imagining cool glassfuls. And when we drink water, we differentiate between chlorinated supplies, the fizz of mineral spring water and the sulphurous tang of spa waters. Our hearts patter faster beside the ozone-laden excitement of waterfalls or crashing waves, and slow down at murmuring riverbanks and quietly lapping shores. Water allows the mind to drift and unfetters the imagination; its fluid nature offers a dream of freedom:

> I must go down to the seas again, to the lonely sea and
> the sky,
> And all I ask is a tall ship and a star to steer her by,
> And the wheel's kick and the wind's song and the white
> sail's shaking,
> And a grey mist on the sea's face, and a grey dawn
> breaking.
>
> (John Masefield, 'Sea Fever')

In many ways, water behaves like a light source.[28] Bodies of water, whether transparent or opaque, shimmer and flicker with constant movement, and are quite literally hypnotic. Any lake, pond or river is a visual magnet, drawing people to sit gazing at the water, mesmerized by its glittering, dancing lights. In conjunction with water's absolute centrality to organic processes, this numinous quality has encouraged human societies to draw associations between water and spiritual being, and to celebrate the beauty of water, in architecture, poetry, art, dance and music.

What we have, then, is a relationship with water that is intensely shaped by its particular material properties, by its essentiality to all aspects of life, and by our phenomenological engagements with it. Because it is so central to our lives, and because its characteristics are so distinctive, water is also one of the major materials that we use in composing ideas. In fact, when we look at this process we discover that, both literally and metaphorically, we 'think with water'.

3   Imaginary Water

Flow

How do we 'think with water'? Nearly half a century ago, Claude Lévi-Strauss observed that people make imaginative use of the material world to develop metaphors. His particular interest was animals, and how they are used to describe certain kinds of behaviour (piggish, wolfish or, for that matter, loyal or noble). 'Animals', he famously said, 'are good to think.'[1] Mary Douglas described how we use our own bodies as a model, for example to describe social bodies (which must similarly have heads, right arms and so on) and landscapes (which have river mouths, cliff faces, necks, shoulders and so forth).[2] Scholars who look at how human cognition has developed over time have described how humans incorporate the material world into their thinking, creating the 'metaphors we live by'.[3]

Water, of course, is everywhere and, though responsive to local conditions, its properties remain constant, as do the sensory and cognitive processes through which humans engage with it. Thus, Ivan Illich says, 'water has a nearly unlimited ability to carry metaphors.'[4] It seems that while each unique cultural context gives people's thoughts a particular shape, the meanings of water have some major cross-cultural undercurrents whose consistencies, not just across cultural boundaries but also over time, are inspired by the characteristics of water itself.[5] This not only helps to explain why ideas such as 'living water' have proved so ubiquitous, and why people everywhere make connections between internal and external hydrological systems,

Leonardo da Vinci's notes and sketches on blood circulation, c. 1508.

it also shows how water can be imaginatively employed to think about other central issues in human life.

Just as the fluid properties of water enable thinking about biological and hydrological processes, water can be used to think about 'flow' in any system. Indeed, it is difficult to think system-ically, or in terms of process, without employing fluid imagery. Before the study of anatomy revealed internal circulatory 'systems', ideas about the body tended to imagine its internal movements in terms of 'ebb and flow'. Though a scholar called Ibn al-Nafis (who died in Cairo in 1288) suspected that blood circulated, the idea didn't take hold until the mid-sixteenth century, at which point ideas about systems and circulation pro-liferated rapidly, leading to the kinds of hydrological and ecological systems thinking explored in the previous chapter.[6]

Water also enlivens ideas about the fluidity of knowledge. Tom McLeish points out that information flows in physical, molecular form, quite literally with water, with 'the embodi-ment of information in matter, and in particular aqueous matter'.[7] But water also provides an ideal metaphor to describe the movement of information, lending itself to images of know-ledge flowing down the generations, or 'circulating' through social connections and a range of communicative media. Like water, knowledge is always in fluid motion: trickling and seeping, permeating, flooding and swamping, even brainwashing. And like water it can be both spiritually moral, flowing from the *fons sapientiae*, or polluting, corrupting innocence and 'poisoning' or disordering.

As well as literally transporting materials around the planet, water also provides a central metaphor for the flow of economic resources. Ideas about economic systems are heavily dependent on images of flow. They move in cycles and waves; they require injections and infusions. Wealth circulates, and may (or may not) 'trickle down'. Markets can be flooded or swamped, or dry up; their indices can be buoyant, or more often (these days) they plunge to new depths. Economies and 'cash flows' are metaphorically 'liquid', thus the global financial crisis was seen as a matter of inadequate 'liquidity':

From August 2007, the *Financial Times* had reported on the serious disruptions and dislocations in global financial markets that were widely represented as a 'liquidity crisis'. This representation was common to practitioner, academic and policy discourse which sought to begin to make sense of the turmoil. It also animated the responses of public authorities. The 'pumping' or 'injecting' of liquidity consistently appeared, for example, as the main motivation behind successive rounds of central bank interventions in 'frozen' money markets.[8]

The literal and metaphorical 'essentiality' of water is similarly evident in thinking about relationships between wealth and power. Power is concerned with agency, the ability to 'make things happen'. In material terms, nothing can happen without water, and thus its meanings as a generative, creative substance are intimately linked with ideas about power and wealth. Water allows individuals, families, kin-groups and whole societies to reproduce, and to produce the things they need and desire. Water 'powers' not only biological but also social and cultural life, enabling processes of material production and so producing the wealth – that is the health and well-being – of those able to direct its flows.

The control of water is therefore essential to political power. In essence, whoever owns or controls the water – the life-stream – is at a very fundamental level in control of events.[9] It is therefore not surprising to find that issues about the ownership, access and control of water create more conflict around the world than just about anything else.[10] And because water is so central to every level of well-being, a society's arrangements about 'who owns the water' provide a precise mirror of both its internal and external political relations. In this sense, the ownership and control of water can be seen as fundamental to democracy, and populations who have lost direct representational control over their most essential resource have, in effect, lost their political power to unelected and often unaccountable bodies.

For most of human history, in most societies, water has been seen as a 'common good': something to which all group members or citizens have a right, and which constitutes collective wealth or well-being – in essence, the 'life-blood' of a coherent social body. This resonates naturally with water's connective qualities. As well as being linked by fluid 'blood ties', communities are also socially, politically and economically connected by their shared use of water, and by shared waterways.

For example, records show that on the River Stour in Dorset, at the time the Domesday Book was written (1086), there were 66 water mills on the river, which is a mere 70 miles in length. Up and down the Stour valley, millers and watermen had to collaborate in managing the flow of water, linking the riparian villages with continual cooperation and social exchange. Similar collective arrangements have characterized water use and management since the earliest Egyptian hydraulic schemes relied on all irrigators to help maintain canal embankments.

Such collaboration is even more vital across societal boundaries. The Jordan; the Colorado; the Mekong: any river that

Water mill on the River Stour, Dorset.

G. Child, 'Canute,
Commands the Waves
of the Sea not to Wet
Him', etching, 1747.

flows across a national boundary has the potential to be a focus of cross-border social and political conflict or collaboration. This underlines a reality that, like biological organisms, societies function less effectively as isolated systems, being reliant on positive interconnections.

Water over time

In a related series of metaphors, water is commonly used to articulate ideas about time. Its capacity to express evanescence is illustrated, for example, in the traditional Chinese practice of writing poems on pavements in water that will evaporate within minutes, underlining a recognition that all states of being are temporary.

With thinking about water and time we also return to an image of water as the 'original' creative potential, the substance from which life arises. What could be more nascent than the 'fountain of youth' represented by a spring? What could be more suited to describing change and transformation over time than the winding flow of water through the physical landscape? Rivers provide a perfect metaphor for the movement of life over time and space: 'springing forth' from unspoiled mountain slopes, they take form in churning energy, waterfalls and rapids that act vigorously on the landscape. The movement of the water is key: Franz Krause observes how, in Finland's Kemi river valley, 'Rapids are so significant to its inhabitants because it is along these stretches of powerful movement that the Kemi is most readily perceived as a "stream of life".'[11]

Growing as they descend, rivers engage with whole eco-systems, absorb other substances and become mature and acculturated through interactions with farming and industry. As many cities are located at their estuaries, they acquire sophisticated cosmopolitan urbanities. Nearing the end of their life journeys they often meander, losing their vitality and 'way'. Finally, they dissolve into formlessness in the sea, until their essence rises, air-borne, to be regenerated in high places. In this way, bringing time and space together in a metaphorical hydrological circle,

The River Wear near Durham Cathedral.

rivers support the hope that what appears to be a finite material journey may indeed continue.

Representing a return to the 'potentiality' of being, the sea inspires both hope and fear. Oceans can open the mind to an image of freedom from material cares: 'I must go down to the seas again', but even this vision is touched with death, implying an escape from the conscious weight of material being. Of course dipping a toe into mortality can be exciting, and peering into the abyss exerts a morbid fascination; to go to sea is to embark upon an adventure spiced with the danger of a journey across 'the deep'. Images of spirit and water rising to the heavens may comfort believers, but for many the sea is 'the great sink' of death, inspiring a genuinely 'mortal fear', of being submerged, subsumed and ultimately dissolved into formlessness. To 'think with' the sea is to contemplate the final dissipation of an individual life-river into oblivion.

The literary canon also contains many allusions to the relationship between water and the loss of conscious memory.

> Far off from these a slow and silent stream
> Lethe the river of oblivion rolls
> Her wat'ry labyrinth, whereof who drinks.
> Forthwith his former state and being forgets,
> Forgets both joy and grief, pleasure and pain.[12]

Lethe was the Greek spirit of forgetfulness and oblivion, and drinking water from the river Lethe, which flowed through Hades around the cave of Hypnos, was believed to induce a complete loss of memory. The Lethe was also called the *Ameles Potamos* ('river of unmindfulness'). As memories were dissolved and the mind liquidated, souls were able to free themselves, forgetting their earlier existence in order to inhabit a new body. Ideas about water, time and loss are enduring, such as in a recent song by J. Ross Goforth, which asks the river Lethe to bring forgetfulness and ease suffering.[13]

The notion of the watery dissolution of the self is not confined to Western classical traditions. In New Zealand, Maori

J. M.W. Turner, *A Storm (Shipwreck)*, watercolour on paper, 1823.

beliefs describe the spirits of the dead making their way towards their origin in Hawaiki, the island home of their ancestors. To reach this they travel along spirit paths to New Zealand's northernmost tip, at Cape Reinga, where the Tasman and Pacific oceans meet. There they 'drink forgetfulness' from the waters of a small stream, and slide down the root of a *pōhutakawa* tree to vanish in a cave that leads into the underworld.[14]

And in a Native Canadian poem by Uvavnuk:

> The great sea
> frees me, moves me,
> as a strong river carries a weed.
> Earth and her strong winds
> move me, take me away,
> and my soul is swept up in joy.[15]

Cultural traditions all around the world and across time are thus redolent with images of final journeys across water into under- or other worlds, regularly dividing human beings hydrologically into the body which may sink into dissolution, and the spirit, which – freed of its mortal coil – can rise into the heavens.

But – perhaps more so in an increasingly secular world – the shoreline is an ambiguous and liminal space, between being and

nothingness. How do people think with wetlands: with places where water, entering marshes, loses its forward momentum?

Sir John Everett Millais, *Ophelia*, 1851–2.

Dichotomous ooze

Hunter-gatherers, intimately familiar with their landscapes and possibly more appreciative of the subtle movements of water through wetlands, have generally seen such regions positively, as rich concentrations of resources. This view has been promulgated more broadly by conservationists, with writers such as Henry David Thoreau and John Muir re-presenting marshy areas as fertile life-making places and havens of biodiversity. With a nod towards their importance as ecosystems, Seamus Heaney describes Irish bogs as 'the vowels of the Earth' in comparison to the hard consonants of dry land.

In other historical periods, though, wetlands have been depicted in more negative and fearful terms as uncanny fluid spaces, filled with untrustworthy bogs and strange miasmas, inhabited by monstrous creatures. This darker view came with transitions away from reliance on wetland resources and Nature-worshipping religions, which 'feminized the swamp positively as the source of new life', towards humanized and masculinized religions and economies focused on dryland agriculture. With more instrumentalist ways of engaging with the environment, wetlands were recast as primal female Nature, requiring masculine control and domestication:

> With the rise of capitalism under the aegis of patriarchy in Europe with its modern cities the black waters of wetlands 'at home' and in the colonies were seen by many citizens as pre-modern wasteland or wilderness to be conquered as a marker of 'Progress'. Wetlands either were drained or filled to create the dead surface of private property on which agricultural and urban development could take place.[16]

Part of the problem too, perhaps, is that wetlands are not really land or water, and ambiguous categories tend to raise anxieties. Slime, neither soil nor water, is similarly uncertain: Sartre had a horror of it, framing it as the feminine opposite of male 'transcendence', and similar revulsion is evident in the work of John Ruskin, whose descriptions of mud-daubed poverty and slime resonate with Victorian disquiet about swamps and their 'miasmas' of disease. John Bunyan's *Pilgrim's Progress* (tellingly subtitled 'from this world to that which is to come') famously provides an account of progress through the 'Slough of Despond'.[17] Many historical visions of hell, such as Dante's *Inferno*, contain foul water and slime, the result of 'stagnation' and the dissolving of solids. The idea that 'civilization' will 'go to hell' in this way is also colourfully described in J. G. Ballard's *The Drowned World*, in which a corrupt and greedy world becomes a putrid swamp.[18] Thus things that are 'corrupt' turn to slime, requiring a further transformation: a separation into fertile soil and clean water, in order to be recycled.

Under mind

The idea that chaos lurks in watery depths recurs in other fluid metaphors. Along with the internal bodily 'hyposeas' that maintain biological cycles, there are other 'seas inside'. A Freudian

Mountaintop wetland at Finse, Norway.

view, for example, depends upon vision of a conscious ego – the ordered, mature and 'formed' self – and the primal, disorderly seas of the unconscious id, which Freud described as 'a chaos, a cauldron full of seething excitations' fed by the instincts.[19] And, according to Jung, in this inner sea, there are what David Gilmore calls the 'chaos monsters': fearsome beings that lurk in the depths of the mind, like the leviathans, krakens and serpents of collective cosmological seas. 'The mind needs monsters', he says, to provide a metaphor for the things humans hope to repudiate.

> It embodies the existential threat to social life, the chaos, atavism, and negativism that symbolizes destructiveness and all other obstacles to order and progress . . . Since Freud's time, we have come to know the monster of the imagination as not simply a political metaphor; but also as a projection of some repressed part of the self. Whether the repressed part is called the id, Thanatos, animus, anima, or instinct . . . the monster of the mind is always the familiar self disguised as the alien Other.[20]

Whether emerging from the ocean's depths, lurking in the ambiguous 'in-between' of wetland swamps, or seen more directly as inhabitants of the inner self, such monsters serve as a reminder that danger and chaos lie under the glittering surface of water.

Heart seas

> Nobody heard him, the dead man,
> But still he lay moaning:
> I was much further out than you thought
> And not waving but drowning.
>
> Poor chap, he always loved larking
> And now he's dead
> It must have been too cold for him his heart gave way,
> They said.
> Oh, no no no, it was too cold always

(Still the dead one lay moaning)
I was much too far out all my life
And not waving but drowning.[21]

The inner seas also flow through the heart, holding its tides of feeling. Not only do the body's physiological responses to emotions express themselves in fluid terms – the flush of blush, the surge of the pulse, the coursing of the blood – water also serves to articulate ideas about what emotions do. Feelings rise and fall, sometimes they flood, running 'out of control', so that we are 'carried away' by them. They ebb, leaving feelings of emptiness. Water's transformative characteristics are particularly helpful in describing how emotions freeze and thaw, heat and cool. In the metaphors through which behaviour is described people may be icy and hard; warm and embracing. Intimacy may be positively 'steamy', and 'inter-course', with its literal fluid exchanges (like those involved in breastfeeding or blood trans-fusion) represents the ultimate flow of life and being across the boundaries of the individual self. To dissolve boundaries and mix fluids is to merge identity and feeling, as Wordsworth put it:

She wept. Life's purple tide began to flow
In languid streams through every thrilling vein;
Dim were my swimming eyes, my pulse beat slow,
And my full heart was swell'd to dear delicious pain.[22]

Just as watery metaphors describe the flow of connections between individuals, broader social relationships can also be evaluated according to the extent to which they can be seen in terms of common substance. Groups are joined in shared iden-tities or separated by a lack of flow. This is most readily evident in language concerned with race and ethnicity, where 'we' are the group composed of shared blood and/or the shared water of a particular place and the 'other' is substantially different. The notion of foreign or 'other'-ness relies on linkage between ideas about substance and identity, in which 'the other' constitutes potential pollution.

'Waves of invasion' are therefore composed of foreign bodies who will 'flood in', 'swamp' and so pollute and disturb an orderly social system, not just with 'other' people's fluid selves (the central concept of miscegenation) but with their flows of 'other' beliefs, knowledges and values. The idea that blood can be tainted is immensely powerful, and such perceived pollution is believed to occur not only through the injection of foreign identities, but also with the taint of criminal pasts, family histories of madness and of course with invasive 'foreign bodies' of germs and viruses which carry polluting 'diseases'.

Based on its particular properties water is thus infused with powerful meanings that connect every aspect of human life, from the microbial flows of individual being to the vast seas of shared cosmologies. As well as providing metaphors that enable us to articulate how we think and feel, these meanings permeate every thought we have about water, every individual, cultural and societal engagement with it. They therefore flow through and shape critical decisions about how water should be used, managed, owned and controlled.

4 Water Journeys

Fluid populations

Water has always been intimately connected to the flow of humans around the world. Early population movements were limited or enabled by the freezing and thawing of water in major ice ages and periods of warming. Over time, groups travelled to new places along the earth's waterways, around its coastlines and, later, across its oceans.

Emerging in Africa 160,000 years ago, populations of *Homo sapiens* first expanded along its watercourses, and then embarked on longer journeys, across the then green and verdant Sahara to the Levant. Their initial forays were pushed back by a global freeze, and in the late Stone Age droughts and other pressures caused an almost critical drop in population levels. It was only after this that human populations were able to grow more steadily and move out of Africa and around the world.

In this move too, water was central, as they sustained themselves through what has been called 'beachcombing' their way along coastlines, making use of wetland and marine resources around the base of Asia.[1] At some point in the Palaeolithic era they began making tentative sea journeys in bamboo or log rafts and dugout canoes, and around 60,000 years ago they reached Australia which, with lower sea levels, was just a small hop across the Lombok Straits from Timor. Frozen out by glaciation, it took another 20 millennia for populations to make it into Europe, and to venture into northern Asia and the Arctic Circle. Then, about

25,000 years ago, moving along coastlines and ice corridors, people crossed the Bering Strait into the Americas.

Throughout this time, human societies lived as hunter-gatherers, adapting to diverse environments with simple stone and then metal tools. Two things were vital to their survival and well-being: water and knowledge. Whether in the form of wetlands, rivers, marine environments or desert springs, traditional hunter-gatherer lives revolved around water sources and the rich diversity of species that these supported. Equally critical was an intimate understanding of local environments and their flora and fauna, as well as their seasonal changes – what resources would appear where and when.

A key area of this knowledge was directly concerned with water: when the rains would come; where to go when there were floods, where to find wells in a dry season, how the rivers and ocean currents flowed, and where aquatic species could be found. Without water storage technologies, a deep understanding of hydrological patterns and even underground flows was essential, and, as outlined previously, these understandings were often used imaginatively, in formulating cosmological models of the world in which water carried human beings in spiritual form out of water sources into the visible world, and then back down into invisible watery domains.

Émile Durkheim famously observed that the religious beliefs of human societies reflect their particular social and political arrangements.[2] Hunter-gatherer societies, generally led by all of their elders, have tended to have similarly egalitarian religious ideas, in which sentient landscapes, as well as being animated by generative waters, contain a multitude of spirit-beings. Like the people themselves, these invariably cluster around water sources, the most resource-rich sites, ensuring that since the earliest stages of human history, springs and their transformative powers have been revered.[3]

Hunter-gatherers' mythologies largely portray animated land and waterscapes as engaging in benevolent and reciprocal partnerships with humankind. They also foreshadow Dante and Freud by many millennia in articulating the ambiguity of water

Aboriginal baptism in
Cape York, Australia.

bodies and their life-giving and life-taking depths. As portals to
a subterranean domain, water places are dangerous, and Australian
Aboriginal stories regularly provide cautionary tales of how
trespassers, or people transgressing ancestral law, have been
swallowed and drowned by angry water serpent beings. Even
today, in many parts of the country, strangers visiting indigenous
homelands must still be baptized with local waters, so that the
ancestral beings in these places will 'know' and not harm them.

The traditional cosmological beliefs of South African !Kung
San people similarly refer to dangerous water beings, such as the
'death giver' !Khwa, 'who is the embodiment of the rain and of
the water in the water hole, his home'.[4] In /Xam mythology,
'death' and 'underwater' are equivalent, and there is a subterranean realm occupied by spirits (*g/amadzi*) and 'monsters' or
'angry things' (*//a:xudzi*) who surface and 'impinge on human
lives when angered by the breaking of certain taboos'.[5]

Hunter-gatherers in Europe shared with those on other
continents a practical and religious focus on wells and springs, and
ancient Britain and Europe contained thousands of sacred wells.
Records of their pre-Roman, pre-Christian uses are sparse, being
provided mostly by Roman military invaders such as Julius Caesar,
or writers such as Pliny and the poet Lucan. However, they do
provide a few accounts of the sacrificial rituals performed at Celtic
wells, and it appears that these were seen to provide access to the

generative powers of primarily female deities. A complementary masculine principle was expressed by the surrounding groves of trees and – possibly – the later stone and wooden henges that echoed their form. At such places, water beings would be both valorized and propitiated to encourage their creative acts and dissuade them from using their powers destructively.

The resonances between the earliest myths of human societies, classical tales of deep water horrors and more recent psychological ideas about the primal id and its lurking monsters powerfully underline the ways that water flows into the human imagination. But in conjunction with these ideas, we can also chart some important changes in how societies have dealt with the balance of power in their practical relationships with water. Hunter-gatherer societies applied only very subtle forms of managerial direction to their material surroundings: some clustering of food and medicine plants around campsites; small and usually temporary fish traps and weirs to improve fish catches and enhance water sources for game; careful cleaning and maintenance of wells and springs. This was a 'light touch' compared to what followed.

Domesticating water

Roughly 10,000 years ago (though at different times in different places), societies began to domesticate animals and plants. Informal cooperation with dogs in hunting, and minor plantings around regular campsites, segued into the creation of temporary 'gardens' in the forest and the corralling of pigs, goats, reindeer or cattle. With the ability to build rafts and canoes, human populations were able to gain access to new parts of the world. For example, the ancestors of the Maori people in the Pacific came from Southeast Asia, via Taiwan, and Lapita pottery locates them in the Bismarck Archipelago to the east of New Guinea about 3,500 years ago.[6] In the first millennium BCE they island-hopped across the Pacific, through Melanesia, New Caledonia, into Fiji, Tonga and Samoa, and possibly across to South America.[7] Travelling in large canoes, carrying seeds,

Traditional stick map from the Marquesas Islands (Te Papa Museum, New Zealand).

plants and animals, they relied on sophisticated abilities to read wind, tides and signs of landfall to find the tiny specks of land scattered across the great blue ocean. By the middle of the thirteenth century CE, a number of canoes had made it as far as New Zealand, establishing legends about a 'Great Fleet' of canoes (*wakas*), each of which is said to have provided the ancestors of a particular tribe or *iwi*.

These ways of making a living were fairly sustainable, although in areas such as New Zealand there was some major deforestation.[8] But then, in some of the world's larger societies, came what Jared Diamond has called 'humanity's worst mistake' – a shift into agriculture. There are alternate views of course: historically, agriculture has generally been seen as 'progress' upon a supposed evolutionary path to civilization. But Diamond is uncompromising, describing farming as 'a catastrophe from which we have never recovered. With agriculture came the gross social and sexual inequality, the disease and despotism, that curse our existence.'[9] In essence, he says, human societies had to choose between limiting growth (which few did), or producing food more intensively and exchanging diversity for fewer but greater quantities of foodstuffs. In most parts of the world there was little pressure to keep population numbers down, as the

Taro garden, Rarotonga, Cook Islands.

burgeoning societies supported by agriculture simply pushed scattered and less numerous hunter-gatherers into marginal land, or overran them entirely, a process that was to continue with later colonial expansions.

Whether a blessing or a curse, agriculture involved a radical change in human relationships with water. At first, wetland areas continued to have a central economic role. In Southeast Asia and Papua New Guinea for instance, Neolithic farming involved subtle water direction in swampy areas to assist the growth of taro. But the crop that provided the most incentive to irrigate more actively was rice, believed to have developed from wild rice plants in the upper Irrawaddy, Mekong and Yangtze rivers.

> The oldest known site connected with intensive rice cultivation is that of Memudu, on the fringes of Lake Taihu, near the mouth of the Yangzi river ... At least 8,000 years ago, the inhabitants of this and neighbouring settlements practised what appears to have been 'receding flood' cultivation of rice on a fairly substantial scale ... using the digging sticks and stone tools available to Neolithic farmers.[10]

This was also the era which brought the rise of hydraulic societies. Along the Tigris and Euphrates in Mesopotamia and the Nile in Egypt, along the Indus in India and the Huang He (Yellow River) in China, farmers began working with the natural cycles of inundation in river systems, charting their rise and fall, and timing their agricultural activities accordingly. Such opportunistic uses of natural floods had little ecological impact, and Karl Butzer observes that along the Nile

> early farming communities continued to use the forested
> riverbanks for settlement sites, grazing animals in the grass
> and bush country of the alluvial flats for eight or nine months
> of the year, and planting their crops on the wet basin soils as
> the floods receded. Big game was still frequent in the Nile, in
> the thickets, and in the 'land of the gazelles', the open country
> or desert, while fowl was abundant along the Nile or in the
> 'papyrus land' – amid the papyrus, reeds and lotus pads of the
> cut-off meanders, back-swamps or deltaic lagoons.[11]

Even low-key manipulation of natural water movements – the building of low bunds, the creation of small channels – was

Irrigated rice terraces in Banaue, Philippines.

labour-intensive: there was a limit to what could be achieved with digging sticks and stone tools. Some societies went on to develop very intricate methods of managing hydrological flows, such as rice terraces, but these too worked in concert with the natural movements of water through the landscape. However, though the environment was only gradually transformed, settlement and a greater reliance on seasonal crops made different kinds of knowledge important, and cosmological ideas adapted accordingly. Many localized spirit-beings remained, but the emphasis shifted to larger deities that not only reflected the more hierarchical social arrangements emerging in agricultural societies, but focused on the interactions between the sun, the moon and hydrological flows.

Earth and Sky

The cosmological ideas of early irrigating societies suggest a deep appreciation of the relationships between celestial bodies and the movements of water between earth and sky. Though origin myths described primeval watery chaos, mythology became more closely concerned with orderly visions of water descending from the sky in annual cycles to fertilize the land and enable crop growth.

For many centuries, through a series of religious transformations and disseminations, the male–female balance evident in the cosmologies of hunter-gatherers was retained. Sun and moon gods such as the Egyptian Ra and the Brahminical Sūrya interacted with rain gods to ensure annual flows of water. The sex of each divinity was not critical, and some were simultaneously female and male. For example, the cult of Tammuz goes back to the earliest Sumerian times. His name, *Dumu-zid-abzu*, means 'the Faithful Son of the Subterranean (fresh water) Ocean', but in late Sumerian liturgies 'he' was also called *Nin-azu*, 'Lord of Healing', *Sataran*, 'the serpent-goddess', and *Ama-ushumgal-anna*, 'the Mother Python of Heaven'.[12]

In the parallel cult of Osiris in Egypt, Osiris was also variously male and female at different times, sometimes being paired with

a female consort Isis, the earth. But s/he is perhaps best described as a more general notion of aquatic potency and fertility, representing 'the vegetation of the Nile valley, which dies in the early summer, when dead is submerged under the life-giving Nile inundation, and comes to life again as the inundation subsides'.[13]

Ancient words and symbols often link water and fertility. Significantly, with the rise of agriculture, there appeared in early Hebrew and Arabic writing a widespread notion of maleness as 'he who irrigates'.[14] The Assyrian cuneiform sign for water was also used to mean 'begetting'. In the Old Testament, the house of Jacob 'came out of the waters of Judah . . . water shall flow from his buckets and his seed shall be in many waters'.[15] The Hebrew term *shangal*, denoting sexual intercourse, resonates with the Arabic *sadjala*, 'to spill water'. And

The ancient Egyptian god Osiris.

in the Qur'an, the word *mâ'un* (water) is also used to describe semen.[16]

Like the primeval origin myths that drew imaginatively on the fluidity of water to conceptualize hydrological creativity, visions of major rain-bringing deities also made use of the characteristics of water and its movements through the world. Like the eternal Ouroboros, such deities were often serpentine beings, flowing in circular patterns of movement. Thus an ancient recitation to Osiris chants: 'Thou art great, thou art green in the name of Great Green Waters; lo, thou art round as the Great Circle.'[17] Francis Huxley compares him to the Celestial Iguana of the Maya:

Seven-headed serpent from a temple in Saigon, Vietnam.

Itzim Na – Itzam meaning Iguana and Na, house or woman – whose name has to do with milk, dew, wax, resin and sap. *Itzam Na* is bisexual, the male principle being in the sky 'in the midst of the waves' while his consort is the unfaithful Earth, goddess of weaving and painting, whose moon-lover yearly emasculates her spouse.[18]

It is not difficult to understand early agricultural societies' predilection for hydrological serpent beings, composed of water and power, cycling between the earth and the sky to create life. The Babylonian Ea; the Indian *Nāga*; the Pueblo 'horned serpent' – all articulate the movements of water on which

Chinese dragon in the
Forbidden City, Beijing.

agriculture depended. In texts such as the *Yih King*, early Chinese
dragons, playing with the celestial pearl/moon, were described as

> a water animal akin [to] the snake which [used] to sleep
> in pools during winter and arises in the spring . . . It is the
> god of thunder, who brings good crops when he appears
> in the rice fields (as rain) or in the sky (as dark and yellow
> clouds), in other words when he makes the rain fertilize
> the ground.[19]

Like the older Australian Rainbow Serpent, many such
beings were linked linguistically with the rainbow. For instance
the Chinese word for rain serpent or dragon, *lyong*, is cognate
with *ghung* (rainbow), *kyung* (bow), *lyung* (arched), *k'ung* (hollow),
lyong (hillock or mound) and *k'yung* (vault, dome). These
linguistic links were echoed in visual form, with the Chinese
dragon typically bent and curved like a bow. Water beings appear
in rainbow form in early art across south and east Asia, for
example in the *makara* of India as a rainbow with a monstrous
head at each end. Chinese versions of this image, with outward
facing heads, also influenced sculptures of sea and rain dragons
in Cambodia and Java.[20]

By working with the hydrological cycles represented by these marvellous beings, the nascent agriculturalists managed to grow a wide range of crops. At Neolithic sites in the Levant, archaeologists have found seeds or chaff from barley, wheat and a range of pulses. Further plant and animal domestications followed as irrigation practices spread, enabling societies to grow flax, beans, maize, cotton, soybeans and rice, and then to cultivate fruits such as dates, figs and olives.

Being intensely dependent upon the annual floods provided by their serpentine rain bringers, and fearful of any withholding of water (or the excessive flows which represented the gods' anger), early irrigators greatly venerated these beings, and the rivers they personified. They made – sometimes human – sacrifices to them, initiating a set of ideas about water bodies' demands for victims that would persist in multiple forms around the world for millennia. Many rivers came to be seen as individual deities: thus, along the Indus, where an early hydraulic society had flourished in about 2600 BCE, the river was regarded as a goddess and mother, and venerated with rituals that continue to the present day.

Such rituals often involved the pouring of libations: thus Pyramid Texts found in fifth and sixth dynasty Egyptian tombs describe how, offered in concert with incantations, libations composed of 'god's fluid' – the waters of the Nile/Osiris – would revive the shrivelled corpse.[21] Like the Celtic 'Green Man' or the Greek sea god Glaucos, Osiris was known as the 'Evergreen One' or 'Green One', and was said to leave green footprints wherever s/he went. Early links between water and eternal life are also evident in the ancient Islamic story of Al-Kidhr's discovery of the Well of Life, which reappears in many myths as the Fountain of Youth.

It is evident, therefore, that the meaning of water as a creative, generative source made a relatively seamless transition from the more localized visions of ancestral spiritual beings common to hunter-gatherers into the larger flood-focused cosmological models of early agricultural societies. And it seems that they also shared rituals expressing a reverence for and a desire to propitiate deities personifying the agency and power of water.

Egyptian goddess in a tree performing a libation ritual, with kneeling woman and ba-bird. Painted decoration on a wooden *shabti* box.

Dam humans

Over time, agricultural productivity, the invention of metal tools and the domestication of cattle, including oxen, opened the sluices to new irrigation technology and more intensive farming. It has been suggested that in the Middle East an additional impetus was provided in about 3000 BCE by regional climate change, in which a pre-dynastic period characterized by frequent rain was followed by increasingly arid conditions.[22]

With the combination of these (and doubtless many other) factors, agricultural societies began to make a key transition into more directive relationships with their environments, and most particularly with water. These changes and further population expansion had concomitant effects on social and political organization, creating wider differentials in power relations. New religious forms reflected these changes, increasingly describing

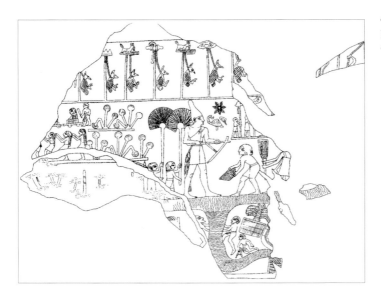

The 'Scorpion King', Narmer mace-head, c. 3100 BCE.

humanized deities, and so implying that agency had passed from animistic non-human beings into human hands.

As irrigation technologies burgeoned, human leaders became more godlike. In ancient Egypt and Babylonia, the king's beneficence was represented in images of him initiating irrigation schemes. Over time he came to be seen not merely as a provider of water to make the desert fertile but as an actual personification of the creative power of water itself. Thus agricultural success and people's well-being were seen as reflective of the king's vitality.[23]

One of the earliest records of irrigation technology, an Egyptian mace-head of around 3050 BCE, shows the Scorpion King cutting the first sod of an irrigation channel. Also depicting a man holding a basket (of seeds) and another holding some ears of corn, the image simultaneously refers to an important ceremony celebrating the annual inundation – a 'day of breaking the river'. This ceremony was still practised in the nineteenth century.[24]

Exerting a further level of human control (or at least providing an illusion of it), the rise and fall of the Nile was measured carefully with Nilometers, stone chambers marked with annual

Nilometer, Elephantine
Island, Egypt.

water levels. These were linked with temples venerating the God
Serapis, who was seen as the originator of inundations of water.

In about 3000 BCE, King Menes built the first dam across the
Nile and simultaneously established himself as the first pharaoh.
Other dams followed, as did more sophisticated irrigation technology. Artificial lakes and canals were constructed. Persian
waterwheels and dams appeared along the Indus, and in China

many stories record the imposition of control over water. A major hero of Chinese antiquity, Yu the Great, was seen to have brought civilization to the region. Reportedly because of his moral virtue, he was given authority by the gods to put the territory in order. His legendary achievement was to redirect the flow of the Huang He, or Yellow River (previously blocked by high mountains), and, eventually, to master all the rivers in China. The political power gained by this harnessing of the water was then demonstrated when he founded the first recorded dynasty, the Xia (2207–1766 BCE) and became China's first ruler.[25]

This illustrates a central point: that the creation of complex irrigation technologies not only imposed greater human control over the material environment and non-human species, but required greater control within human societies to manage both the shared infrastructure and the larger and more concentrated populations enabled by intensive food production.

Large infrastructural arrangements required management and cooperation. By creating laws such as the Code of Hammurabi, a major codification of Sumerian and Babylonian law inscribed on stele in 1772 BCE, irrigating societies began to require citizens to take on collective responsibilities for maintaining canal embankments and dredging channels. With these arrangements came more regional political arrangements, and more powerful leaders. And it was with these kinds of changes that the polytheistic religions populated by both male and female gods began to give way, in the most populated parts of the world, to visions of supreme leadership and patriarchal monotheism.

Patriarchal waters

> Almighty God! no hand but thine
> Can check this flowing tide;
> Stretch out thine arm of power divine,
> And bid the flood subside.[26]

Early Judaeo-Christian and Arabic texts demonstrate a series of transitions in which diverse gods and prophets were set aside in favour of an omnipresent, all-powerful and, in the end, singular male being. The ancient flood stories in both religious traditions retained a notion of watery chaos and disorder, but were re-framed in terms of an all-powerful God expressing punitive and then forgiving powers. In such texts, the leviathan water serpents so central to previous religious traditions began to be seen not as powerful (albeit dangerous) creative beings, but in much more negative terms, as disorder itself.

Increasingly, in the larger, more powerful societies, the material world became feminized Nature, as opposed to human (male) Culture. This bifurcation presented a very different sense of order to the previous, more integrated cosmologies, in which non-humankind, including the waters of the world, had been seen as working in partnership with humanity. Recast as 'other', the non-human was seen as requiring human (and male) dominion. There was chaotic water – the out-of-control floods that resisted containment – and 'good' water: rains that came at the right time and in the right quantities, and water arriving as needed in controlled irrigation channels. Thus the vision of paradise that dominated increasingly monotheistic religious texts is one of a controlled and carefully watered agricultural garden:

> Yahwist myths are concerned with irrigation and production – God 'planted a garden in Eden', 'a river arises out of Eden, watering the whole garden'... Yahweh God took the human and placed him in the garden of Eden to work it and to care for it.[27]

And it was the patriarchal humanized God who provided this water and maintained authority over it, wresting power away from the former deities of Nature. Both the Bible and the Qur'an are full of images in which water is provided through His bene-ficence, flowing down from the Temple to fertilize productive endeavours, to cleanse and purify, and – in the later narratives – to bring spiritual wisdom and rational enlightenment.

It will be apparent from this account that each religious and material relationship with water built on previous ideas, incorporating and reshaping them. Monotheistic religions arrived in concert with water management practices that were increasingly directive and instrumentalist. With both cosmological and material power and agency placed squarely in human hands, it became imperative to quell earlier and now subversive ideas about non-human powers.

A spate of serpent slaying followed. Originating in earlier Babylonian and Mesopotamian 'combat myths' in which the great leviathans of early chaos were dispatched, these stories describe (usually) male culture heroes – morally superior warriors whose task it was to demonstrate human authority over the recalcitrant and sinful powers of Nature both internally and externally. St George and St Michael are the most obvious examples, appearing in multiple images either slaughtering serpents or 'heretics', but many early Christian saints also won their spurs by slaying dragons. And these stories followed the path of monotheism as it permeated different parts of the world, for example producing the Norse Sigurd and of course Beowulf; the Greek Heracles; in Persian mythology, a hero called Mithra; and in Indian texts, Krishna and Aghasura.[28]

In the plethora of visual and narrative imagery depicting these heroic deeds, these serpents, including the serpent in the Garden of Eden, are often portrayed as female. In this way, as an

St George from a 15th-century illuminated manuscript, the Bruges Garter Book.

Krishna kills the serpent
Aghasura, 1675–1700.

image of Nature, and of the religious traditions that venerated non-human deities, the serpentine water being came to stand for subaltern and (in monotheistic terms) pagan beliefs. During the course of biblical narrative development it was cast, increasingly, as the embodiment of evil. In the medieval period – resonating with ideas about death and dissolution – the serpent was often represented not only as the leviathan rising from the deeps, but also as the 'mouth of hell' that would swallow souls on the Day of Judgement. This alignment of ideas has by no means vanished: in *The Satanic Bible*, published in 1969, the leviathan still represents the element of water and its potential for both creativity and destruction.[29]

The coalescence of ideas that conceptualized Nature and particularly water as female came hand in hand with the assertion of male authority in religious, social and political arrangements, in relationships with the material world, and most especially in relation to water. Irrigation therefore enabled – and was enabled by – a new cosmological vision of human dominion.

5 Redirections

Seductive powers

Early irrigation schemes represented a quantum leap in human societies' capacities to control their material environments and support larger populations. To be able to direct the element of life itself, to impound and so 'own' it, was also intensely seductive. It is not hard to understand the allure of dams and channels: the satisfaction of watering crops and seeing green shoots appear, the ability to 'garden the world' whether on the grand scale of farming or in small domestic spaces.[1] Once people began to engage in a more directive manner with water there was an almost inevitable impetus to do more and more: to build bigger dams and canals; to direct the flow of events. Indeed, it could reasonably be said that the control of water, more than anything else, changed humankind's relationship with the other species on Earth and asserted the primacy of human agency.

Such power was also potentially competitive; rivers could be dammed and withheld from enemies downstream or with godlike powers released in a punitive flood upon them.[2] An Assyrian king, Sennacherib (r. 705–681 BCE), dammed the Euphrates in order to let loose a flood upon Babylon.[3] 'To me Sennacherib King of Assyria to do this work by the will of God to my attention was brought and important it became.'[4] Sennacherib was also a skilled water engineer and invented water-lifting machines that enabled the planting of cotton in Assyria. He made green gardens, irrigated vast plantations and gave people 'beautiful wells'. He wasn't shy about his achievements either, recording on a cuneiform tablet how, in Nineveh,

> Eighteen rivers I caused to be dug; to the midst of the river Husur (Khosr) I caused to be directed, and their channel from the boundaries of the city Kisir to the midst of the Nineveh, the river with an excavation I excavated; their waters I brought down within it . . . I brought the strength of these waters from the midst of the land of Taz, mountains difficult on the frontiers of Acad within my country . . . On the stones of that river 'the opening of Sennacherib' I recorded its name . . . the river Khosr I caused to be directed, and their channel to Nineveh, a stronghold supreme, the seat of my royalty from a distance I brought.[5]

However, irrigating from rivers with massive annual inundations was not always successful. The groups that settled along the Indus between 3000 and 1500 BCE built a highly sophisticated system of water management and sanitation: a Great Bath still considered by water engineers to be extraordinary;[6] reservoirs, canal irrigation; wells in every third house and public baths. Rain gauges appeared first in India, and records show careful consideration of rainfall patterns and soil types in devising cropping arrangements. There was also, in a treatise on administration called the *Arthasastra of Kautilya*, a body of Water Law. But the Indus, like other rivers prone to large annual floods, changed its course and irrigators found (as did those in Mesopotamia) that irrigation required more and more labour to maintain embankments and prevent channels silting up, and that it created salination that was poisonous to crops.[7]

The tenuousness of human control was also revealed when events went more dramatically awry. The Qur'an records the bursting of the Marib dam in Yemen in about 400 BCE. Built between 1000 and 700 BCE, this had been regarded as one of the wonders of the world, but God could still be punitive: 'The people of Seba had beautiful gardens with good fruit. Then the people turned away from God, and to punish them,

Ancient *noria*
at Hama, Syria.

The Pont du Gard, Provence, built by the ancient Romans, was 50 km in length and carried water from a spring at Uzès to the Roman colony of Nemausus (Nîmes).

He burst the dam, turning the good gardens into gardens bearing bitter fruit.'[8]

In some ways, irrigation systems were easier to build in areas where annual water flows were less volatile. Small-scale technology could also be quite effective, even in arid regions. For example, in the first millennium BCE, considerable agricultural success was achieved in Egypt and contiguous areas through the widespread use of *qanāts*, which drew water from hillsides with a series of vertical well shafts connecting underground tunnels. And in the seventh century Persian waterwheels, *noria*s, made a major impact on water management.

More temperate areas with higher population densities required larger-scale water supply systems, particularly as – at around 600 BCE – the first urban societies began to emerge in the Mediterranean region. Equally empowering in such societies was the capacity to harness the strength of water to do work previously requiring massive amounts of human labour. With sectors of the population not only freed from food production but enriched to the point of having considerable leisure, the flow of water into the cities also enabled a flow of ideas, including scientific experimentation and the development of even more sophisticated technology.

This much more directive engagement with water was exemplified by the early Romans who, having conquered large territories and acquired a multitude of slaves in the process, constructed some of the world's most impressive aqueducts. In 312 BCE Appius Claudius Caecus built the first of these, Aqua Appia, and the next couple of centuries saw, across the Roman Empire, a massive building programme not only of aqueducts and underground channels, but of sewage systems, roads and harbours.

Between 27 and 17 BCE one of Rome's most famous water engineers, Marcus Vitruvius Pollio, wrote a treatise, *De Architectura*, which offered advice on how to find water and made use of Greek theories about hydrological cycles to speculate on the sources of hot and cold springs. He also recorded some of the engineering knowledge emerging at the time, which produced water clocks and siphons, as well as waterwheels and Archimedes screws for lifting water out of mines.

Vitruvius' work was foundational to that of Sextus Julius Frontinus (*c.* 40–103 CE), whose text, *De Aquaeductu*, reported to the emperor on the aqueducts of Rome, describing the water

Michael Zeno Diemer (1867–1939), *Wasserleitungen in altem Rom* (Restored Aqueducts of Rome).

supply system in detail, including the sources of water as well as the size of each channel and its discharge rates. The text also laid out the laws relating to the use and maintenance of the system, and noted the tendencies of local farmers and tradespeople to tap into the system illegally.[9] Critically, the development of Roman law laid the foundations for more individual ideas about property and the privatization of water resources.[10]

The capacity to deliver water into cities had a range of effects, not least in making 'the metropolis' possible. Equally important to the flow of water into cities was the ability to discharge waste. Rome had the Great Sewer, the *Cloaca Maxima* (whose name was then given homologously to animals' excretory orifices). Constructed to drain marshes and remove effluent, this also brought a higher standard of living, leading Dionysius of Halicarnassus, writing in the first century BCE, to proffer the opinion that

> The three most significant works of Rome, in which the greatness of her empire is best seen, are the aqueducts, the paved roads, and the construction of sewers . . . Water is brought into the city through aqueducts in such quantities that veritable rivers flow through the city and the sewers.[11]

Roman water users also paid attention to the quality of their water and the particular characteristics of each water source, and were averse to blending them. Aqueduct channels were separated from each other as much as possible, and Pliny the Elder reported that the Aqua Virgo, which supplied the Trevi Fountain in Rome, 'refused to mingle with the waters of a nearby stream sacred to Hercules, and therefore was named Virgin'. Clearly ideas about purity and pollution were meaningful even then and Cassiodorus, a Roman senator who lived from about 490 to 585, observed that 'Purest and most delightful of all streams glides along the Aqua Virgo, so named because no defilement ever stains it.'[12]

The effectiveness of its aqueducts and underground channels was such that Rome had a higher amount of water available per capita in the classical era than is possible in many contemporary cities. Water was stored in high cisterns (*castella*) and linked with outlets via a network of lead pipes. Wealthy homes had indoor plumbing, and there were many elaborate fountains which, as well as providing public and private drinking water, celebrated the power of water and the wealth and prestige of Rome.

Like the monarchs in ancient Middle Eastern palaces, wealthy Romans expressed their elite status through their ownership of private and often decoratively sumptuous water wells and fountains, and through the luxurious use of water in their homes, providing a material reminder of the symbolic meaning and practical reality of water as a source of wealth and power. The relationship between water and power became increasingly evident as the ability to direct water flows not only enabled enlarged agricultural capacity but allowed technologically sophisticated societies to develop new forms of production.

Canopus at Hadrian's Villa in Tivoli, Italy, *c.* 130 CE.

Once unleashed in temperate climates with numerous waterways, water power began to gather momentum. The ability to

replace human and animal muscle with mechanical power radically changed people's ways of thinking about water, work and Nature.[13] It also permitted conquerors to control populations with technology as well as with military force, introducing new productive practices into colonized societies. For example, following the Romans' early colonization and enslavement of Celtic tribes in Britain, the Norman invasion subjugated the indigenous population, and this was due in part to the economic expansion created by a massive increase in the number of waterwheels and mills. The Domesday Book (1086) records over 6,000 such mills in England, milling corn and flour and making paper and cloth.

With increasingly industrial forms of production such as iron working, the harnessing of water power was soon a major driver of growth, firmly establishing a more utilitarian way of engaging with water and the wider environment. There began a trend which has continued ever since, in which more mechanized forms of agricultural production required fewer and fewer agricultural workers, while the burgeoning factories of industry served to pull people away from rural lives into the cities.

A combination of greater productivity and expanding populations created inevitable pressures for spatial expansion. More specialized products, for example minerals or cotton, also needed wider trade relations. Nascent states, coalescing around regions, monarchies and religions, therefore reached outwards exploratively, commercially and hegemonically, to the lands inhabited by smaller, less powerful societies, subsistence farmers, pastoralists and hunter-gatherers, seeking resources and land for settlement. In these endeavours as well, water, and the ability to cross the seas and travel along waterways, was critical.

Waterborne connections

Between 500 and 200 BCE Arab traders sailed to west India's Malabar coasts and the Chinese to North Vietnam. Malay and Indonesian shipping carried goods to the Bay of Bengal, and capitalized on a growing trade from India to Rome. In the later

Reconstructed water wheel at L'Abbaye de Fontenay, near Dijon, France.

centuries of the first millennium CE, the Vikings made longship forays across the cold northern seas.

In warmer climes, the Straits of Malacca and the southern Java Sea became key centres of wealth as Europeans sought Asian spices. Many luxury goods came overland, via caravan, but sea and river routes gained importance, particularly as the amount of trade increased. The Red Sea ports of Mocha and Aden fed Indian Ocean commodities into Europe and Asia Minor and, in the first millennium CE, the Tang and Song dynasties in China encouraged trade with Europe and the newly emerging Muslim societies.[14]

The requirement for accessible ports and ways to transport goods to these placed a new emphasis on rivers and particularly their estuaries. For example, the lower Mekong delta developed into a major trading centre, and a process began in which river estuaries around the world became the focus of urban settlement.

Maritime trade did not merely exchange goods of course: people and ideas also flowed along trade and military routes. Important cultural dialogues developed between China and India, the Middle East and Europe, enabling the spread of Islam.[15] Sea trade brought Muslim enclaves to Java and Sumatra, and the first Muslim states appeared in about 1200. By the 1500s there were sultanates in the Malay Peninsula and Islamic empires in Persia, India, Iraq, Syria and Egypt, and this flow of Islamic faith across the oceans continued until the Portuguese conquest of Malacca in 1511 imposed Christian beliefs in the region.

Christianity had started in pockets across the Levant, and spread rapidly across northern Africa and Europe. Following the Portuguese oceanic voyages along the Atlantic coast in 1418, and Vasco da Gama's successful expedition to India in 1498, this new religion reached into the furthest corners of the world over the next two centuries. Expeditions had religious, political and economic aims, and there were increasingly competitive seaborne excursions in which the Portuguese, Spanish, French, English and Dutch navies vied for control of the oceans and the new continents that they connected.

Naval commanders circumnavigated land masses, reporting on their topography, their harbours and what could be gleaned about their shorelines, their flora and fauna, and their human inhabitants. Once landfalls had been made, explorers made their way up major river systems into continental interiors to report back on their resources and to assess their prospects for trade and/or colonial settlement.

Woodblock of
a poem by Fujiwara
no Toshiyuki Ason,
with scene showing
junk gliding near
shores of Sumi,
by Katsushika
Hokusai, *c.* 1835.

Sea scapes

The colonial outreach of large agricultural societies initiated a
different kind of relationship with the sea. Previously, mainly
land-based Christians had retained a view of the oceans as
dangerously chaotic: 'Tertullian, a third-century Church father,
believed that water was highly attractive to demons and the Devil
. . . The sea was seen to be evidence of the unfinished nature of
creation; a primeval remnant engendering a strong sense of repul-
sion.'[16] But this changed in the medieval period. By the end of
the first millennium populations in Europe were enlarging
rapidly and, despite being radically checked by plague in the
1300s, their continued growth created an ever greater impetus for
expansion. The nascent scientific thinking, which had been so
important in thinking about water as a substance, also led to new
ways of understanding ocean currents, tides and winds. New
forms of cartography and inventive navigational technologies enabled Magellan to undertake the first recorded circumnavigation

97

of the earth in 1519. The sea became infinitely more traversable, yet continued to provide some barrier to invasion. As Thomas Churchill at the outset of his *Life of Lord Viscount Nelson* (1808) declared, the ocean 'affords not only the most ready and convenient medium of intercourse between remote parts of the globe,

Sea serpent, woodcut from Olaus Magnus's *History of the Nordic Peoples* (1555).

but the means of annoying an enemy with the most facility, and at the same time the securest protection'.[17]

Even with more robust vessels and the new understandings of ocean travel, seafaring remained fraught with danger and ambiguity. There were storms to weather, and persistent fears about lurking malevolence in the ocean's dark depths. Sailors imagined monsters rising to swallow them up; accounts of sea voyages contained numerous sightings of sea serpents, and charts regularly depicted such creatures.[18]

Many of these themes were still evident in 1798 when, inspired by tales of early sea journeys, Samuel Taylor Coleridge published 'The Rime of the Ancient Mariner', with its strange meld of ancient superstitions, supernatural events and Christian salvation. The poem communicates the terror of the storm-blast 'tyrannous and strong' and the sense of frozen entrapment when 'the ice was all between'. It also highlights the contrast between the primal salt water, and the sweet fresh water with the verse that famously encapsulates the idea of thirst:

Water, water, every where,
And all the boards did shrink;
Water, water, every where,
Nor any drop to drink.

This agony of thirst also brings to the surface the terror of mortal dissolution in the savage ocean, and a classic revulsion about the ambiguity of 'slimy things . . . upon the slimy sea'.

Published just 60 years later, Herman Melville's classic *Moby-Dick; or, The Whale* provides a different view of the sea and its creatures. There are still some potential terrors in the depths. Captain Ahab seeks revenge upon the white whale that had both destroyed his boat and bitten off his leg. To him, the whale is evil and malevolent, although a crew member tries to persuade him that 'Moby Dick seeks thee not. It is thou, thou, that madly seekest him.'[19] In this sense, the whale stands both for the dark inner impulses of the unconscious, and the externalized terrors of the deep. But at a

William Strang, 'And Now the Storm Blast Came', illustration of Samuel Taylor Coleridge's 'The Rime of the Ancient Mariner', 1896.

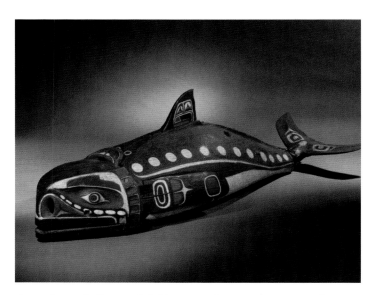

Kwakwaka'wakw whale
mask, British Columbia,
19th-century.

time when whaling and fishing were becoming major industries,
the novel also reflects a much greater ability to dominate the seas.

Not that whaling was new: even in prehistoric times, coastal
hunter-gatherers such as the Ainu, the Inuit, Native Americans
and (in the first millennium) Basques had gone out in small
boats to hunt pilot whales, belugas and narwhal, driving them
onto beaches, or using harpoons with drogue anchors to tire
them out. Ancient rock carvings show even large whales, sperm
whales, humpbacks and Pacific right whales hemmed in by
boats. Whales also feature centrally in Maori traditions, as illustrated most recently by the story of *Whale Rider*, in which the
whale (one of Maori cosmology's many important underwater
beings) appears as the guardian spirit of the tribe.[20] But though
pre-industrial societies recognized that such creatures were dangerous, like the Aboriginal rainbow serpents, they were seen as
largely benign powers, totemic beings that could be celebrated
in art and performance.

While totemic value and use as an economic resource were
compatible in small-scale economies, a quite different relationship with aquatic species was engendered by a commercial whaling and fishing industry that sought whales not as occasional

Destruction of Leviathan,
Gustave Doré, 1865,
engraving.

feasts but as a source of materials (whalebone and oil) on an
industrial scale. In Europe, along with larger oceanic explorations,
more intensive forms of whaling were developed in the 1500s
and, despite Inuit resistance, whaling stations were established
by Basques in Labrador, Newfoundland and Iceland. Whaling
and fishing in Arctic fisheries continued, with increasing com-
petitiveness, until well into the seventeenth century, by which
point the whaling industry was dominated by British, Dutch
and (in the Pacific) Japanese vessels, who continued whaling on
a large scale until the First World War.

Subsuming flows

Whaling is both a metaphorical and literal illustration of the way that larger industrializing societies 'conquered' the powers of the sea. Naval power was critical in the sixteenth and seventeenth centuries as nations fought for supremacy in controlling sea routes, fisheries and access to the 'New World'. Charts of these early explorations were closely guarded secrets, as were the details gleaned about ocean currents, coastlines and the different character of seas, winds and weather around the world. Such knowledge was empowering, providing competitive advantage for societies as well as transforming the deep and infinite unknown into knowable, controllable waterscapes.

Influxes from expanding societies also brought radically different relationships with water into cultural landscapes where smaller societies had maintained less intensive and more collaborative ways of working with their material environments. In Africa, the Americas, Australia, the Pacific and in the colder northern regions, clans of hunter-gatherers, tribes of cattle farmers, reindeer herders and subsistence farmers felt the impact of maritime forays whose purpose was exploration and trade or – where there were major disparities in military power – direct colonization.

As had happened with earlier invasions in Europe, the latter brought new technologies of production. Indigenous peoples, when not simply exterminated, were bundled into reserve areas, required by missionaries to learn horticulture, or forced to provide labour for settlers intent upon clearing land and establishing agricultural and pastoral enterprises. As colonial settlements spread upriver into continents, the indigenous groups long clustered around rich estuarine wetlands were forced to retreat further and further into deep green interiors, or into harsh and marginal desert areas, while the coastal swamps that had previously supported diverse resource uses were drained to create new agricultural farmland.

In this way, much more directive ways of engaging with fresh water were borne by salt water to every continent, subsuming the water worlds of their long-term inhabitants. Irrigation and farming methods developed in temperate climates were exported to arid regions such as California and Australia. And, inevitably, the prime sites in any new colonial environment were always the freshwater lakes and river, the sources of wealth and power. The seizing of these enabled colonial governments to impose their ideas on the indigenous groups who – willingly or not – became subjects of the Crown.

As well as requiring them to adopt new economic practices, this subjugation also demanded that indigenous populations be 'educated' in new ways of understanding and evaluating the world in both religious and secular terms. In missions and schools across colonial empires, long-term Nature religions that valorized sentient ancestral landscapes and polytheistic notions of spirit-inhabited trees and rivers were dismissed as primitive superstition, to be replaced by patriarchal and monotheistic religious beliefs and the emergent scientific understandings of the global north. And so particular beliefs about the rightful 'dominion' of man-kind – ideas about 'progress', growth and development, and instrumental values concerned with 'making Nature productive' – took their first steps towards globalization.

6 The Power of Industry

National pursuits

The coalescence of power and the mechanisms of government necessary to create nation states and empires were intimately linked to hydraulic development. Examples abound: in China, following the dynasty-establishing water direction of Yu the Great, imperial expansion depended on irrigation systems to intensify agriculture and a system of canals to transport grain to the capital.[1] But upholding imperial power in this way also meant maintaining increasingly demanding infrastructure.

Like the Mesopotamian irrigators before them, Chinese engineers discovered that such systems were enormously labour-intensive and time-consuming. Canals caved in and silted up; land eroded and salinated. Distribution arrangements broke down under the pressure of intensification and social conflict, and water flows ceased to be able to meet increasing demands. Impacts on ecosystems affected the viability of other (often more long-standing) forms of resource use, such as fishing, harvesting wet-land resources, or collecting marine species. As irrigation systems failed, so too did political power. In China, 'by the late Imperial period (c. 1500) hydraulic breakdown, followed by rehabilitation of control systems, followed again by hydraulic breakdown were components of a cycle that occurred with increasing regularity.'[2]

Similar patterns recurred elsewhere. In fourteenth-century Bengal, for example, Ahmed Kamal describes how the Mughal sultanates relied on power and prosperity acquired through major irrigation. 'Ibn Batuta travelled from Sylhet to Sonargaon by

Canal in the Forbidden
City, Beijing.

boat, and observed orchards, water-wheels, prosperous villages
and gardens on both sides of the rivers, as if he was passing
through a market.'[3] The sultanates' schemes were carefully organized, with public works departments devolving funds to local
landlords (*zamindars*) who, in return for managing canals and
embankments, were allowed to tax the peasants. However, this
relatively stable traditional system faltered under the disruption
of the Afghan wars of 1794, and then crumbled further under
British rule which, focusing mainly on collecting revenues, failed
to invest in maintenance or to accommodate local social and
ecological realities.

Nevertheless, hydraulic development remained central to the
creation of the centralized governments that, in many parts of the
world, were establishing nation states and shifting the emphasis
from cultural and religious affiliations to new forms of national
identity. Their hegemonic expansions to colonial areas added a
new dimension to their engagements with water. They began, on
an increasingly grand scale, to import water from elsewhere in
the form of the goods produced by water use in colonial regions.
This established a critical pattern of externalizing the social and
ecological costs of production, enabling powerful nations – at the
expense of the less powerful – to compensate for the insufficien-
cies created by internally unsustainable levels of growth.

Inner city flows

Robert Hyde Colebrooke, *Benares: View of the City from the Water*, c. 1792, pen and black ink, with grey wash and watercolour.

The rising population densities that, from the Middle Ages onwards, provided the impetus for colonial appropriation also drove rapid urban expansion. As it had for the early Greeks and Romans on a smaller scale, the modern clustering of people and nascent industries into major cities presented two key problems: how to bring in sufficient (and sufficiently potable) water supplies, and how to get rid of domestic and industrial wastes. Both of these challenges were to have radical effects on people's relationships with water and with each other.

Until this time most people had collected domestic water from village wells, which also functioned as important focal points for meeting and socializing. Small-scale water supply systems required fairly undemanding technology: channels, water pipes made from hollowed logs or lead, waterwheels and simple pumping mechanisms. With relatively small clusters of people and cottage industries, the use of nearby waterways as drains for sewage and other wastes, though not ideal, was sufficiently low-key that local ecosystems could absorb the effluent without major difficulties. But the expansion of cities all over Europe created challenges to human and environmental health on a very different scale.

Cities were necessarily situated where there were good water sources. The Romans had originally chosen the site of Londinium, for example, because there were two tributaries, the Fleet and the Walbrook. There were terraces of water-bearing gravel and a number of natural springs. But London's population, like that of other European cities, doubled in the thirteenth century, probably

Stalbridge village pump, Dorset.

reaching over 50,000. 'The problem was not lack of water, but generation of urban wastes.'[4]

Open gutters, known as kennels, received not just the contents of domestic chamber pots, rubbish and ashes, but also the dung of domestic animals. Some rubbish was put into pits in tenements, but as these cut into the water-bearing gravels, their run-off went into the waterways anyway, to 'pester the river with fylthe and muck'.[5] Domestic dwellings had stone-lined privy pits, but these were costly to empty and often overflowed. People living beside streams built privies emptying straight into them. Also directly into the watercourses went new and particularly noxious industrial wastes, such as the effluent from tanning factories (which used animal faeces in curing leather) and butcheries (which produced bloody 'shambles'). Consequently water supplies in the city became so vile that people drank 'brewed' ale, beer or wine instead.

Just as wetlands had been devalued and increasingly perceived as rotting, unhealthy places with the rise of agriculture, the ambiguous water supplies of medieval cities raised anxieties about health, being seen as the source of the poisonous air or 'miasmas' believed to cause disease. In 1290 a group of Carmelites in London complained to the king that 'putrid exhalations' from the mouth of the Fleet had caused the deaths of a number of friars.[6] But despite the passing of numerous laws and increasingly draconian measures to prevent dumping and pollution, London festered. It became necessary to pipe water from springs further afield, and following the building of the king's 'Great Conduit' in the thirteenth century, a number of new channels were constructed to bring water from afar.[7]

The pollution of urban waterways resuscitated ideas about 'bad', life-threatening water. Once again, base, out-of-control Nature must be disciplined into good behaviour by the imposition of human agency, in this case expressed through new kinds of water treatment and more sophisticated forms of delivery. Like the channelling of irrigation supplies, these technologies further affirmed an idea of water as the product of Culture rather than Nature.

A vision of water as something that had to be 'denatured' and re-produced by human actions had a further impact in that it crystallized a shift in ideas about ownership. The building of irrigation infrastructure had established the idea that water could be owned by a regional or imperial power. Similarly, the development of urban water supplies required major investments of labour, technology and expertise.

As the Romans had discovered with their aqueducts, and the early hydraulic societies with their canals, urban water systems also required complex forms of governance that defined who owned which supply sources, who would have access and when, and who would pay and be paid for water delivery. In London, as in other cities, there was much toing and froing about who was responsible for water supply and infrastructural maintenance, with tasks and responsibilities being the subject of an ongoing tug of war between municipal agencies, philanthropists and private investors.

Previously, the Church had been the main provider of water to those dwelling in the vicinity of its wealthy and powerful abbeys. This had forged an important link between the supply of

Old butcher shop in Cloth Fair, West Smithfield, London, etching, 1790–1820.

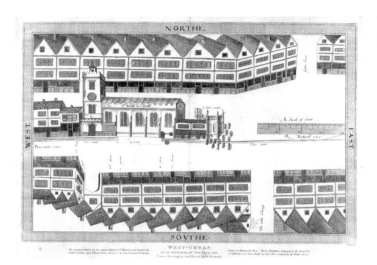

The King's Conduit and old buildings in West Cheap (Cheapside), London, drawn by Ralph Treswell in 1585, here in a 19th-century copy.

water and ideas about moral leadership. What could be more morally authoritative, after all, than the dispensation of the stuff of life, the substance of the spirit, the symbolic cleanser of sins? What could be more indicative of moral turpitude – and more deserving of punishing disease – than the wallowing in chaotic Nature represented by inadequate sanitation? So contests over the ownership and control of city water supplies were not only concerned with political power and economic profit, but also with moral leadership and an ongoing contest for primacy between Church and State.

Widening social divisions were also expressed by access to water in the city. The rich were literally 'in the loop', with their houses tapped directly into piped water supplies. There were people who, though not wealthy, could afford to pay water carriers. The poor – who composed the majority – simply lugged water from wells and standpipes themselves, and had little influence on the provision of supplies, unless they resorted to becoming 'water stealers', siphoning water covertly from the new supply pipes.

Remaking the rivers

Control over the flow of water was not only vital within cities, but also in ensuring fluid connections between urban and rural areas. In Europe, prior to the industrial age, canals – first introduced by the Romans – were fairly limited, hand-dug (in their case slave-dug) channels, branching out from springs and rivers for the purposes of local irrigation, or constructed to drain wetlands and enlarge agricultural areas.

Even with the development of larger irrigation schemes, the initial focus was mainly on watering nearby fields to grow crops or create water meadows (which meant that the season for grass growing was lengthened and also produced rich pastures).[8] The building of major churches, monasteries and castles in the medieval and early modern period, together with the need

Fountains Abbey, North Yorkshire.

to transport stone and timber, had led to some canalization of rivers, but these newly navigable watercourses remained, for several centuries, the only alternative to packhorses and oxen.

With industrialization, however, the aim became not merely to cut irrigating capillaries from local waterways, or straighten short sections of river, but to make great arteries of water that would enable the movement of substantial quantities of goods around the country. The first major canal, dug by the Duke of Bridgewater to carry coal from his mines to Manchester in 1761, is said to have fuelled the Industrial Revolution. There followed, between the 1770s and the 1830s, a 'golden age' of canals, in which goods and people moved with increasing ease.

Peter Perez Burdett after Jean-Jacques Rousseau, *View of the Barton aqueduct of the Bridgewater canal,* *c.* 1772–3.

> Some water projects represent truly dramatic changes in history, e.g., the Hoover Dam in the USA, the Aswan dam in Egypt and Sudan, the Duke of Bridgewater canal in England or the Emperor canal in China. When implemented they changed the course of development in the locality and beyond.[9]

Critically, the 'golden age' of canals in Europe coincided with rapid advances in the development of steam engines. Just as the fluidity of water had enabled channels for irrigation and the movement of people and goods, just as its flowing energy had turned water wheels and mills, water's particular properties came into play again, as its capacity to be transformed into steam provided the pressure to power steam engines.

This underlines how the properties of water are braided through each stage of human engagement with it, both limiting and enabling societies' activities. Writing about 'the remaking of the Colombia River', Richard White thus presents the river as an 'organic machine': an energy system that, although modified by people, retains its own 'unmade' qualities and does its own work, which links with that of humans. As he puts it:

> The world is in motion. Tectonic plates drift across a spinning planet. Mountains are lifted up and eroded to the sea. Glaciers advance and retreat. All natural features move, but few natural features move as obviously as rivers. Our metaphors for rivers are all metaphors for movement: they run and roll and flow . . . Like us, rivers work. They absorb and emit energy; they rearrange the world.[10]

None of the diverse cultural ways of life enabled by irrigation or by water transport could have happened without water's particular physical properties, and this is equally true of the steam that powered industrial development. At the same time, however, steam power made this a more unequal relationship, freeing societies from some of the physical constraints of water. Steam boats could go against the current and, for nineteenth-century Americans, 'machines stood as both the agents and symbols of their conquest of nature', playing a central role in an epic struggle towards 'progress'.[11]

The transition from water and horsepower to steam also led to the decline of the briefly vital canal system, which was rapidly superseded by the development of railways which were faster to build, easier to maintain and more flexible than canals.

Steamships shrank distances further, and fast and powerful transport across the seas was further speeded by the building of the Suez Canal in 1869. International flows of trade and exchange reached a whole new level.

In essence, all of the developments enabled by water made the world itself more fluid, permitting the rapid movement of goods and people between continents and across them. Previously self-contained cultural contexts, though often radically altered by colonial interventions, became more permeable, more open to exchanges of people, material culture and ideas. It became possible, at least for wealthy elites, to be cosmopolitan, to circulate through different cultural milieux, and to have wider, cross-cultural conversations.

Making H_2O

A key global conversation was that concerned with science. Scholars had been exchanging ideas for many centuries, but radically increased movement and communication around the world produced a commensurately larger and more coherent flow of information. The seeds of scientific analysis of the elements planted by the ancient Greeks came to fruition in the eighteenth century. Over the next century this led to ways of thinking about material things that, combined with much greater technical capacity to 'engineer' the world, produced a relationship with water and ecology that was fundamentally managerial. Notions of spiritual immanence or forces that permeated and animated all things, which had persisted through myriad changes in religious forms, were finally extracted, making God literally immaterial. Ivan Illich describes scientific visions of ecology as 'the death of nature':

> With the Scientific Revolution . . . a mechanistic model came to dominate thinking. As the object of man's will, nature was transformed into dead material. This death of nature, I would argue, was the most far-reaching effect of the radical change in man's vision of the universe.[12]

The opening of the
Suez Canal, 1869.

A techno-managerial view of the world contained considerable hubris about human abilities to direct events, encouraging the idea that anything could be deconstructed and reconstructed in accord with human desires: waterways, landscapes, farms and cities, as well as humans, animals and plants. Though many religious beliefs proved resistant to scientific materialism, defending their visions of water and spiritual being, such ideas were increasingly pushed to the margins. Science came to dominate public discourses, and by the late nineteenth century water had become thoroughly domesticated in Europe, both intellectually and physically. In London, given a hearty shove by the 'Great Stink' that fouled the air in 1858, advances in water engineering, combined with Victorian philanthropy and investment, created a florescence of new water infrastructure that roundly proclaimed the triumph of human agency.

Sizeable reservoirs were built, along with beautifully decorated pumping stations celebrating both the power and status of water supply. Water mains full of pressure, capillary pipes leading into domestic dwellings, and vast catacombs of brick-lined

'Father Thames
Introducing His
Offspring to the
Fair City of London',
Cartoon from *Punch*,
3 July 1858.

sewers finally solved the intractable problems of urban water
supply and sanitation. Now all city dwellers could enjoy the
luxury of water piped into the home, available at the turn of a
tap. And, with an awareness of the science and technology
underlying these privileges, all could appreciate this flow as the
product of human agency.

Achieving distinction

The more cosmopolitan social world that pertained in cities was
very different from that of long-term village-scale communities
related by blood, place and history. Living mobile urban lives,
people were less able to build ideas of common place and sub -
stance with others. Surrounded by thousands of strangers, they
became more conscious of boundary-crossing bodily smells and
substances. Anxieties about the potential pollution and invasion
of the self – always psychologically powerful – came to the surface,
and more individuated notions of the person emerged, requiring
containment and defence. It became more important to achieve
'distinction'.[13]

New scientific knowledge about germs and waterborne disease transmission further heightened these concerns, encouraging

a commitment to 'hygiene' and to cleansing the self and the home. Adequate sanitation for all became a symbol of 'civilization', and a reliable flow of water in domestic spaces therefore became necessary to the maintenance of individual and familial integrity: a defence against invasive forms of otherness. Jean-Pierre Goubert notes that 'when Queen Victoria came to the throne in 1837, there was not a single bathroom in the whole of Buckingham Palace.'[14] But by 1882 Eardley Bailey Denton was able to claim that:

> It is now generally acknowledged that a dwelling cannot be considered as complete without a bathroom, and that its adoption should not be limited to the superior mansions of the wealthy, but that all classes of our population should ... benefit by the comfort, cleanliness and healthfulness afforded by both hot and cold baths.[15]

As this implies, though, there was no loosening of the connection between water and status. Having luxurious bathrooms and washing facilities, using them more and, above all, using more water, achieved immediate relevance as the epitome of wealth and social success.

While washing became more important all round, it was particularly so for women. The images of nude women bathing, much beloved by painters of the time, continued to conflate women and subversive 'irrational' Nature, but in the late nineteenth century a new 'hygienic' image of women emerged, which represented an ideal in which both water and flesh were safely and intimately domesticated.[16] This idealization helped to obscure the anxiety-generating realities of public water supplies as a chemically adulterated substance further compromised by contact with – and possibly carrying traces of – the substance of others:

> The intertwining of urban water and the nude constitutes one of the strands of a taboo woven to protect the symbolism of public water from analysis ... we do not feel free to question the natural beauty of water itself because we know,

Mary Cassatt, *Woman Bathing*, 1890–91.

yet cannot bear to acknowledge, that this 'stuff' is recycled toilet flush.[17]

Healing water

Emergent notions of hygiene, bodily integrity and cultural control over internal and external nature had a major effect on ideas about health and water. Concepts of health – in a variety of cultural forms – depend on physiological, emotional and mental processes flowing in an orderly fashion, maintaining proper balances, undisturbed by material, intellectual or moral pollution.

Through a more scientific lens, these views, like those of external ecosystems, became more mechanistic in their form, remaking the body in engineering and chemical terms as structures, materials and processes enabled by the flow of water and nutrition through a series of pumps, valves and pipes. In this materialistic vision of order, inner health could be achieved by imbibing 'the right stuff', initiating a much closer interest in the material 'purity' and healthful composition of food and water.

As a result, the holy wells and sparkling springs that, through multiple social and religious transitions, had supported both moral and physical health via the 'spiritual' potency of water, became transformed into 'spas' in which the mineral and chemical contents of the water were regarded as the primary health-giving ingredients. Precise information was given to imbibers about the various minerals in the water and how these would improve their health.

Social 'distinction' was therefore achieved by access to water supercharged with healthful substances and, in eighteenth- and nineteenth-century Europe, the upper classes developed considerable enthusiasm for 'taking the waters'. Health spas, located in charming gardens with fountains and music, became key social gathering places by offering both mineral drinking water and curative baths. Taking inspiration from early Greek and Roman enthusiasm for such practices,[18] balneologic societies sprang up, and held 'balneology congresses'. With world travellers bringing tales of ancient Native American and Scandinavian traditions, saunas became popular too, along with other 'water cures'.

Spa water in Karlovy (Karlsbad), Czech Republic.

There was a related flurry of interest in cleansing with salts. Historically, the 'everlasting' qualities of salt had given it both religious and medical importance in a range of cultural contexts.[19] It was used by Greeks and Arabs to welcome guests; by the Romans to affirm friendship and acquire wisdom; by the Vikings to embalm chieftains slain in battle; and by early Christians to purify and nourish, 'keep the Devil out' and ward off witchcraft. Salt's long history as a positive substance provided a useful background to new 'scientific' ideas about health and the efficacy of mineral purges to rid the body of 'the wrong stuff'. Epsom salts, having been investigated scientifically by Torbern Olof Bergmen in Uppsala, gained widespread popularity for their purgative (one might say purgatorial) properties. Saline water was used in efforts to combat cholera in the 1800s, and a new set of ideas arose about the benefits of bathing in salt water. Numerous seaside 'health resorts' appeared, with modest bathing machines allowing women to enter the sea demurely. Like the mineral health spas, these enabled new forms of social co-mingling via water.

Congregating around water, or sharing immersion in it, therefore became an important new way of making connections between people, reframing water places as sites for leisure and relaxation.[20] Rivers too became the focus of new leisure activities in Europe, rehabilitating a previously ambivalent relationship with them.

During early modern times, rivers were considered dangerous
. . . Children were warned to stay away from rivers and their
treacherous currents . . . Coroner's records from the sixteenth
century show that as many as 53 per cent of all accidental
deaths were caused by drowning.[21]

Prior to being tamed by engineering schemes, rivers had
been seen as uncontrolled fluid spaces, lacking social control.
'Water language', like 'gutter language', was a term for swearing.
But rivers were (perhaps because of this) an early focus for 'leisure',
a concept of free time that emerged in the fourteenth century.
The year 1496 saw the publication of *Treatyse of Fysshynge Wyth
an Angle*, purportedly written by Dame Juliana Berners. And Izaak
Walton's *Compleat Angler*, published in 1653, was regarded as one
of the most important English books ever written, with only the
Bible and the Book of Common Prayer reprinted more often.

As riparian areas were developed, river bathing became safer
and more popular, and new ideas emerged about health, the body
and recreation. Swimming came to be seen as healthful activity,
highlighting the meanings inherent in 're-creation', which is conceptually founded on ideas about the renewal or re-making of
the self.[22] This fitted seamlessly with ideas about the body and
how this too could be maintained through health and leisure.
Thus, according to *The Compleat Swimmer* (1658), both the nature
of the body and the body of Nature could be purposefully controlled, and water became incorporated into a human-engineered
vision of the body, the self and wider material systems.

7 Engineering Utopia

Underneath the fountain

Water has always been an object of contemplation and affective engagement, and every development in water technology has brought with it artistic expressions celebrating water's aesthetic qualities. Carved stone basins for collecting water date back to ancient Sumeria at around 2000 BCE; the earliest aqueducts culminated in decorated fountains; and in 600 BCE Athens centred on a fountain called the Enneakrounos, which supplied drinking water to the local populace through nine spouts.

However, it is from the Roman *fontis/fontem* (spring) that we get the word 'fountain', whose central theme of water as life and as the substance of social connection carries through into the 'fonts' used to baptize newcomers into religious congregations. In ancient Rome, at the time of Sextus Julius Frontinus, aqueducts fed 39 monumental fountains and nearly 600 public basins, and there were innumerable private fountains in the courtyards of wealthy Roman families and the imperial household. While Greek fountains often depicted the water emerging from the mouths of animals, Roman preferences were for human figures to supply this precious substance, underlining their more assertive ideas about the human control of water.

In the medieval and early modern periods, fountains were strongly associated with ideas about paradise, a word which itself comes from the Persian *pairi-daeza* for 'enclosed space'. This referred to the Islamic walled gardens of the seventh century. In these, the four rivers of paradise (represented by four channels

Mosaic panel from a Roman fountain, showing the sea god Oceanus, with water streaming from his mouth, 3rd century CE.

of water) flowed from a fountain in the centre which represented the spring Salsabil, the Qur'anic source of water.[1]

It also became conventional to build fountains alongside mosques so that worshippers could purify themselves through ritual washing before entering the temple. The vast Ottoman Empire helped to disseminate this practice further, and the fountain at the Temple Mount in Jerusalem was built during the reign of Suleiman the Magnificent. The design of Islamic gardens was highly influential, appearing in the designs of the Mughal Empire in India, and echoed in the Shalimar Gardens in Lahore, built by the Emperor Shah Jehan in the 1600s.

Underlining the flow of ideas between the emerging mono-theistic religions, similar water imagery characterizes descriptions of the Garden of Eden. Illuminated manuscripts such as *Les Très Riches Heures du Duc de Berry* (1411–16) depict elegant gothic fountains in heavenly gardens. In the cloisters of the great Christian abbeys, intended to represent these havens, it became common to have a central fountain illustrated with allegorical stories praising the saints and prophets. Like the earlier Islamic fountains, these were also used for ritual washing to purify the body prior to worship.

The more earthly generative powers of water were similarly celebrated in medieval *jardins d'amour* (gardens of courtly love), which provided enclosed spaces for romance. Such gardens abounded with jolly ejaculatory streams, as described in the medieval *Roman de la Rose* (1470), whose illustrations depict a fountain and a stream pouring outwards from the centre of the garden.

Whether directed towards imperial, religious or secular meanings, fountains provided a consistent affirmation of water

Leonardo Dati, *The Fountain of Life*, miniature from *De Sphaera*, c. 1450–65.

Postage stamp
of Shalimar Gardens,
Pakistan.

as the stuff of life, health and wealth, and as a source of power. Those who controlled and so 'provided' water could see their power reflected in it: thus, like the other baroque fountains added when Rome's aqueducts were restored in the 1700s, the Trevi fountain provided clean water to the populace through the grace of His Holiness the Pope. By this time, greater mechanical sophistication had made very elaborate fountains possible. Rulers keen to express their sovereign powers flaunted these in energetically spouting artworks. For example, Louis xiv's fountains at Versailles, built in the late seventeenth century, were created as a testament to the authority of the *Ancien Régime* over both Culture and Nature.

Such potent spoutings have continued to provide powerful expressions of national identity. No capital city is complete without an impressive central water feature and, like the equally unsubtle international competitions to have the tallest skyscraper, having the largest water jet provides an ultimate symbol of the ability to generate wealth and power. The 140-m high *Jet d'Eau* in Lake Geneva (created in 1951) held the title for some time, but has since been out-spouted by King Fahd's

Fountain in Jeddah, Saudi Arabia, which shoots water 260 m into the air.

Illustration from the medieval French poem *Roman de la Rose*, c. 1300s.

Since the eighteenth century, competitive municipal aspirations have echoed those of national rulers. Many city fathers built massive parks with intricate fountains, including musical fountains that would spurt and spray in time to loud renditions of classical music compositions.[2]

The celebration of water power evident in architecture and landscape design was reflected in other art forms. Handel's *Water Music* was written for George I, and first performed for him in 1717 on a barge on the River Thames. More recently, there is Maurice Ravel's *Jeux d'Eau* (The Fountain/Water Games, 1901), Claude Debussy's *La Mer* (The Sea) and his *Reflets dans l'eau* (Reflections in the Water, 1905). Poems have long celebrated water's beauty too.

Who has not often spent long hours by the ocean
When it lay spread at his feet, without ripple or motion,

Contemplating dreamily the picture of wonder
That smiled in the sunlight the blue mirror under![3]

Similar veneration has also run through the visual arts, valorizing the properties of water, exploring its beauty and articulating the meanings attached to it.

As industrializing societies democratized and became more affluent, wealthy individuals followed their leaders and surrounded

Fountain at Versailles.

Musical fountain, Budapest.

their manorial houses with parklands, lakes and fountains. Since the eighteenth century, social aspirants have demonstrated their membership of the upper classes by 'holding' great lakes of water in carefully landscaped parklands and constructing beautified springs and grottoes containing frequent visual references to classical figures and their associated powers.

Claude Monet, *Water Lilies*, 1908.

Like the Italian Renaissance gardens that inspired them (with their echoes of medieval heavenly gardens), these aristocratic landscapes often contained ideas about spiritual journeys to the source or fountain. A classic example is provided by Stourhead in Wiltshire, where Sir Henry Hoare commissioned a garden in which paths take the visitor on a journey through Arcadian woods, via temples, to an 'underground' cavern guarded by a river god. Here in the tufa-lined cave is the source of the River Stour.[4] A classical nymph reclines beside a limpid pool, at which a poem reads:

> Nymph of the grot, these sacred springs I keep,
> And to the murmur of the waters sleep
> Ah spare my slumbers, gently tread the cave
> And drink in silence, or in silence lave.

Developing water

While the aesthetic qualities and generative powers of water were being celebrated artistically with joyful fountains, its abilities to turn economic engines were also being fully utilized. Steam turbines freed production from direct dependence on waterways. By the beginning of the nineteenth century, the industrial revolution was spinning faster, pushing its productive activities worldwide with centrifugal force.

Stourhead, Wiltshire.

ss *Potsdam*, c. 1852.

The twentieth century dawned, for some, with enormous confidence and optimism, and for others with considerable disruption and dislocation. Industrialized societies now had the capacity not only to travel with relative ease to the furthest reaches of the globe, but also to embark on ambitious programmes of social and material engineering in which water was the most vital ingredient. A very muscular notion of development had taken hold. Evolutionary ideas had placed humankind squarely on a path in which industrialization and conforming to its various social and political accoutrements were seen as the apogee of 'progress'. The corollary was an expectation that the entire world, and its ecosystems, would be regulated by 'intelligent man'.[5]

Major social changes are always reflected in water. The programmes of water engineering that took place in the twentieth century precisely illustrate the ideas about social and ecological relations that directed events. In the colonies of European nations, environments were required to be ever more amenable and productive, thus meeting Edward Said's definition of imperialism as 'an act of geographical violence through which virtually every space in the world is explored, charted, and finally brought under control'.[6]

Waterways were therefore transformed into 'imperial water', and expected to conform to ideas about hydrological flows historically rooted, for the most part, in temperate geographic areas where aridity was regarded as inferior and 'uncivilized'.[7] The idea that aridity was morally inferior hugely influenced colonial development. For example, in the American West and Australia, having displaced the indigenous people, settlers set about trying to 'green the desert'.[8]

Such efforts were driven by visions of a well-watered Utopia in which water, Nature and people were brought under control and into productive service. In Australia, for example, these ideas were manifested through engineering water in ways that, unlike the subtle indigenous management that had proved sustainable for 60,000 years, were radically directive. Boreholes punctured the Great Artesian Basin like a pin cushion, growing in number so fast that its levels fell, requiring ever deeper wells. Farm dams pockmarked the land's surface to provide reservoirs for cattle in the dry season. Then, as technical capacities increased, massive engineering projects were undertaken to dam rivers and initiate major irrigation schemes.

Like the religious conversions of indigenous people, these were missionary efforts. Thus Ernestine Hill's account of early irrigation in Australia (aptly named *Water into Gold: The Taming of the Mighty Murray River*), describes a moral crusade:

> the transfiguration of a continent by irrigational science. The miracle . . . in the drought-stricken Murray River Valley, has already, by example, inspired the stupendous, national schemes for water preservation, conservation, allocation, that are changing the face of Australia today.
>
> The invisible and illimitable waters of Australia are now being revealed and redeemed . . . The vast artesian basins, the 'silent' rivers and lakes vanishing, the sweeping floods lost in

sea and sand, can all be saved, unveiling a New Australia to our eyes.[9]

With chapter titles such as 'Apostles of Irrigation', 'Utopia on the Murray' and 'Acts of God', Hill's message was clear: if Australia was recalcitrant in providing sufficiently reliable water for progress, zealous engineering and scientific 'expertise' would persuade it to do so. Like the medieval serpent slayers, water engineers were cast as culture heroes, whose task it was to subdue the big rivers winding across the landscape. And, like the earlier dragon slayers, they were usually men, placing the management and control of water firmly in male hands.

The idea of a dam

There is perhaps no human invention that so fully expresses power over the material world as a dam. To stem the flow of the substance of life; to channel it into the service of human endeavours: what could provide a clearer statement of control? More to the point, to believe that societies have the right to do this offers an ideological vision of human–environmental relations that sits in contrast to earlier, more collaborative arrangements with other species and material environments. For instance, Jamie Linton observes that although the Romans built magnificent dams and aqueducts, they were wary of impeding the flow of water.

> The waters of the aqueducts flowed freely from the fountains and baths of Rome, through the streets of the city and into the Tiber River. There were no taps, no technical means of stopping these waters. Nor was this merely a matter of failure to invent the valve; respect for water demanded that allowing it to flow remained 'a necessary condition of its proper use'.[10]

Roman law actively forbade the containment of aqueduct water: *Aqua currit et debet currere ut currere solebat* ('water may be used as it flows and only as it flows'). The Romans were clearly proud of their accomplishments, as seen with Frontinus' famous boast,

The Hoover Dam.

'With such an array of indispensable structures carrying so many waters, compare, if you will, the idle Pyramids or the use-less, though famous, works of the Greeks!' But, like other societies at that time, Romans saw the world and its animating forces as existing on relatively egalitarian terms with humankind.

This was not the case with the irrigators of the early twenti-eth century, who entertained few doubts about their rights to build massive water impoundment schemes to achieve their progressive aims. Nor were these confined to putatively 'virgin' landscapes. Many low-key 'traditional' irrigation schemes which had functioned sustainably for centuries were replaced by more radically directive arrangements.

'May you cultivate below a furrow'[11]

An illustration is provided by Mattias Tagseth's description of how, in Tanzania, the slopes of Mount Kilimanjaro have long provided a 'green oasis' of water in an otherwise arid area, sup-porting Chagga smallholders' agricultural and agroforestry efforts with a system of gravity-fed *mfongo* canals. Managed by tribal leaders and framed by cosmological beliefs and rituals in which the construction of irrigation furrows was tied to the bringing of rain, this intensive but low-key system permitted stable and fairly self-sufficient cultivation and produced a diverse range of crops: 'the kihamba plot may contain more than one hundred different useful plants, of which bananas, coffee, beans and root crops are the most important ones.'[12]

Such systems, though, can only be sustained at a certain level, and are vulnerable to pressures for growth. Population expansion led to some fragmentation of the farms, and to out-migration, which affected the community's social stability. Introduced cosmological ideas subsumed the detailed local knowledges and beliefs foundational to traditional water management. School attendance and conversions to Christianity weakened adherence to canal rites and the mystical ideas surrounding the schemes.

In the 1930s, the Chaggas and their *mfongo* irrigation scheme were pushed aside as other groups competed for Mount

Kilimanjaro's water. Plans were made for hydropower development and for larger, industrial-scale irrigation schemes, oriented towards producing tradable monocultural crops rather than diverse self-sufficiency. In the late twentieth century, mandatory water licences were introduced 'to limit what was seen as waste of water, and to reform the "deficient" organization of irrigation by peasants'.[13]

This example typifies how, in colonial societies around the world, as well as in the independent nations that emerged subsequently, irrigation and then hydroelectric power became intimately connected to the business of nation building, of centralizing political power and of competing politically and economically at an international level. A utilitarian vision of water and the language of science were essential to this process, upholding a discourse which 'makes the association of dams and development seem only natural'.[14] But the more fundamental meanings of water remain central too: holding water is holding power, life and generative potency. Thus the bigger the dam, the bigger the nation.

One of the first 'mega' hydroelectric dam schemes was the Hoover Dam, built near Las Vegas on the Colorado River during the American Depression.[15] Rising 220 m above the river, it provided employment for thousands and cost nearly 200 lives. It was named as one of the Top Ten Construction Achievements of the Twentieth Century by industry professionals in 1999, and is now a National Historic Landmark. At the dedication of the dam in 1935, the u.s. Interior Secretary Harold Ickes was unequivocal about its purpose: 'Pridefully, man acclaims his conquest of nature.' Supplying 90 per cent of the water for Las Vegas, the dam now provides water and power to about 25 million people.

Similar national pride was inspired in Australia by the Snowy Mountains hydroelectricity and irrigation scheme. Between 1949 and 1974 major dams, reservoirs and pumping stations were built, radically transforming the region and playing an important role in establishing Australia's cultural and economic independence.

In China in 1927, the Nationalist government attempted to recentralize administration partly by establishing the Huai

River Conservancy Commission to promote 'modern' hydraulic practices. This focus on large water projects coincided with many such endeavours in the USSR and USA, reflecting 'the muscular ability of governments to . . . rearrange the natural environment in order to promote agricultural and industrial development . . . [and] to engineer economic growth and, thus, political legitimacy'.[16]

In the same way that the national pride expressed in major public fountains was replicated in local water features, the literally monumental dams being constructed at a national level in industrialized countries were echoed in state and farm irrigation schemes. Waterways everywhere were assessed in terms of their suitability for the construction of reservoirs, and their potential

effects of displacement: 'landlessness, joblessness, homelessness, marginalization, food insecurity, increased morbidity, loss of access to common property resources, and social disarticulation'.[3] Such disruptions are particularly disempowering to rural women, often increasing the labour required to maintain health and hygiene in a domestic context, and demanding economic practices that widen inequalities in gender relations.[4]

In the last few decades international opposition to major dam building and water-diversion schemes has grown, with conservation and human rights organizations becoming increasingly vocal, and specific groups, such as the International Rivers Network and the European Rivers Network, springing up to defend waterways. In 1997, in response to this oppositional pressure, the World Commission on Dams (WCD) was established 'to protect dam-affected people and the environment, and ensure that the benefits from dams are more equitably distributed'.[5] Though not challenging a broader developmental agenda, the Commission stated that while the benefits derived from dams have been considerable, 'In too many cases an unacceptable and often unnecessary price has been paid to secure those benefits, especially in social and environmental terms, by people displaced, by communities downstream, by taxpayers and by the natural environment.'[6] Although many countries have become more equivocal about dams, some – for example India, China, South Korea and some African nations – remain heavily committed to further development along these lines.

As in the colonial era, when the major aim was to settle unruly indigenous populations, avoid famine and develop a lucrative revenue base, irrigation in these contexts is still presented in what Gerardo Halsema and Linden Vincent call 'the political discourse of a benevolent paternal state that should modernize society by imposing new systems of justice, fairness and equity'.[7]

In effect, such 'modernization' entails a shift from local ways of managing water and resource distribution, often refined over centuries, to more centralized managerial arrangements. Numerous ethnographers have recorded how delicately balanced traditional knowledge and ways of managing shared water resources have been disrupted by the imposition of more development-oriented governance.

A classic example is provided by water temples in Bali, where a long-standing traditional system combines religious beliefs and tribal social arrangements and empowers village priests to manage an intricate system of hydrological flows through rice terraces. Stephen Lansing's work has shown how increased government control and the promotion of developmental aims, along with 'scientific' methods of boosting production, rapidly proved less sustainable, overriding carefully balanced social reciprocities and failing to engage with the complexities of local ecosystems.[8]

In India national independence came hand in hand with Nehru's statement that 'dams are the temples of modern India.' Since the 1970s there have been ongoing battles between dam proponents and opponents, and major social, political and legal controversies continue to dog the Narmada Valley Development Project. Largely without consulting the 1.5 million people who would be displaced, the government proposed 30 large, 135 medium and 3,000 small dams on the Narmada River and its tributaries.[9] According to the Friends of the River Narmada,

Pura Ulun Danu, Balinese water temple.

Sardar Sarovar Dam
on the Narmada river,
India.

The proponents of the dam claim that this plan would
provide large amounts of water and electricity which are
desperately required for the purposes of development . . .
However, once one cuts through all the rhetoric, lies and
subterfuge of the vested interests, the gross inequities
are clear. Large numbers of poor and underprivileged
communities (mostly tribals and dalits) are being
dispossessed of their livelihood and even their ways of
living to make way for dams being built on the basis
of incredibly dubious claims of common benefit and
'national interest'.[10]

Author Arundhati Roy has also been passionately critical of
the scheme:

Big Dams are to a Nation's 'Development' what Nuclear
Bombs are to its Military Arsenal. They're both weapons
of mass destruction . . . They represent the severing of the
link, not just the link – the understanding – between
human beings and the planet they live on. They scramble
the intelligence that connects eggs to hens, milk to cows,

food to forests, water to rivers, air to life and the Earth
to human existence.[11]

The redirection of water into industrial production also highlights the tensions between notions of inherited rights in water
commons, and the recreation of water as a saleable commodity.
For example, also in India, there have been major controversies
during the last decade over Coca-Cola's vast bottling plants in
Plachimada, Kerala, in the Sivaganga district in Tamil Nadu,
and in Kaladera, Rajasthan. Court battles continue, with community action groups arguing that the company's water use has
massively reduced or contaminated groundwater levels in contiguous areas, in practical terms appropriating the long-term
water rights of local farmers.[12]

Widespread protests have also been mounted (though
with less effect) against China's Three Gorges dams. Massively
impounding the Yangtze River in 2009 with barriers five times
the size of the Hoover Dam, the project is expected to displace
several million people.[13] And whether on major river systems or
on smaller waterways, the costs of dams are by no means borne
only by human populations. In the Yangtze River the loss of the
rare freshwater baiji dolphin (also known as the Goddess of the
River) is only one of many such examples. Along with the sub-
sumption of swathes of river valley and forest, dams disrupt the
normal movements of rivers to which local species have adapted.

Radical alterations to water flow can be catastrophic for
aquatic species and those dependent upon them. Dams prevent
silt from replenishing fertile delta areas, and nutrients from
reaching marine life. 'Scouring' water releases flush through
dried (and thus vulnerable) valleys, removing river beds and banks
and creating erosion which compromises water quality both in
rivers and coastal ecosystems. Without fish ladders, dams prevent the upriver travel for spawning necessary to many fish
species.

The human and other species downstream from dams are
also at risk in other ways. The creation of major reservoirs
increases the risk of seismic activity in a region, as well as adding

an additional risk of flooding should the dam be affected by this or other events. There have been quite a few major dam failures, most often following heavy rains, or due to construction weaknesses, and dams are now marked on maps with the three orange dots that denote sites categorized in International Humanitarian Law as 'installations containing dangerous forces'.

Scarcely water

Although such massive impoundments of water have taken place, population movements from rural areas to urban slums, and insufficient water in some areas, means that approximately a billion people lack secure drinking water supplies and more than twice that number have inadequate sanitation provision. The redirection of water into human activities has also had major impacts on its quality, and here too the world's poor take the brunt of the impacts, with 10,000 to 14,000 people (mostly children) dying each day from waterborne diseases.[14] There are vast inequities in these arrangements: the plastic bottles of clean spring water that seem to have become prosthetic extensions to the hands of Western teenagers take six times the amount of water to produce than they contain.[15]

'Riverside' dwellings in Manila, Philippines.

Water's capacity to dissolve and carry other substances means that all flora and fauna share the costs of pollution. One of the most widespread ecological problems resulting from dams and irrigation has been the salination of massive areas of land. The regular watering of shallow-rooted crops raises water tables and brings salts to the surface, poisoning the soil and rendering it infertile even to native vegetation. Much irrigation depends on pumping out groundwaters too. Not only are these finite, as aquifers take centuries to recharge, but many also contain salts and other minerals that have negative impacts on soil structures. Just as the efforts of earlier agricultural regimes to 'green the desert' failed because of salination, today salinity is a major issue in Israel, the Middle East, the USA and Australia. In the latter, for example, what farmers call 'the white death' currently affects more than 5 million hectares of land and this is expected to more than triple in the next 50 years.[16]

Salinated land in Etosha Pan, part of the Kalahari Basin, Namibia.

Pollution is also worsened by lower flows in rivers. Impound-ments and overabstraction prevent the annual flushes that in many rivers previously removed detritus and carried silt and heavier pollutants out to sea. Low flows also mean less dilution of any salts and pollutants in waterways; thus – although efforts are now being made to address this issue – by the time it reaches Mexico, the Colorado River has long been reduced to a saline trickle, leaving Mexican farmers with only 'liquid death' to pour over their prime agricultural land.[17]

Despite regulatory efforts to protect riparian areas, indus-trial farming methods have released a flow of chemicals and other pollutants into watercourses. Many modern crops depend not only on the use of herbicides and pesticides (with the com-mensurate disappearance of whole populations of plants and insects),[18] but also on the heavy use of fertilizers which, by adding excessive nutrients to waterways, have radical effects on weed growth and can also cause eutrophication, a lack of

Since 1970 the International Tanker Owners Pollution Federation (ITOPF) has recorded over 10,000 oil spills.

oxygen in the water.[19] Added to this is the nutrient-rich slurry from intensive dairy farms located in the rich water meadows found alongside rivers.

Coral reef in the Red Sea.

The opposite problem is caused by acid rain from airborne industrial emissions, which can impede aquatic plant growth. As well as devastating forests, this has created, in parts of Canada and Europe, 'dead' lakes where only foul algae (*mougeotia*, or 'elephant snot') will grow. With so many pressures on aquatic ecosystems, and continued drainage to extend farmland, the

International Union for the Conservation of Nature (IUCN) predicts that 41 per cent of the world's amphibian species will be forced into extinction in the next half century.[20]

Everything ends both metaphorically and literally in the sea, of course, and here the effects of pollution are keenly felt in delicate marine ecosystems. With sewage outlets still pumping millions of tonnes of human waste into the ocean; with heavy metals from industry shifting downriver and out of estuaries with every dredge; with oil spills and other chemical catastrophes occurring with depressing regularity, there are multiple pressures on marine ecosystems. On shoreline after shoreline the sea grasses and other aquatic plants that supported multiple species are disappearing and small biota are choking. With pollution, and with the effects of rising temperatures and changing sea levels, coral reefs, the colourful kaleidoscopes that took millennia to grow are greying and dying to the extent that the IUCN anticipates that by the middle of the twenty-first century almost all of them will have disappeared.[21]

Euripides said that 'the sea can wash away all evils', but although many societies have believed historically that 'the great sink' has an infinite capacity to absorb, cleanse and regenerate, today, more than ever, this is a dangerous illusion.[22]

Undermining water

Material pollution is not the only pressure on marine environments. Noise pollution – 'acoustic smog' – is affecting all the species that rely on echolocation to communicate with each other and to find their way around the oceans. As the polar ice cap has shrunk, opening up the Northwest Passage, there has been rapid growth in northern shipping. Engine noise, seismic mapping of the continental shelf and gas exploration have massively increased the levels of underwater noise at the frequencies used for echolocation by whales and dolphins.[23]

Mining is, in any case, one of the most water-polluting industries and it is currently booming worldwide to feed rising industrial demands for minerals. Alluvial excavations strip

A beached harbour porpoise at Norderney, Germany.

riverbanks and create massive increases in water turbidity. Almost all mining requires large amounts of water for washing ore and, despite the efforts of environmental regulators, mining discharges remain a major source of pollution. Particularly virulent is the use of substances such as cyanide to extract minerals from ore which, though theoretically contained in tailings dams, regularly leach into watercourses over time. As politicians say, 'everything leaks eventually'.

Mining activities have significant impacts on downstream water users and ecosystems, but the industry often occupies a pole position in national economic aspirations, and transnational mining companies enjoy commensurately warm relationships with centralized government bodies. They are thus able – even encouraged – to forge ahead with the expansion of their activities. Reporting on mining in the headwaters of the Ok Tedi River in Papua New Guinea, Stuart Kirsch observes that such disparities in power lead to major abuses of human rights.[24] There is a plethora of similar examples around the world: the aggressive expansion of mining since the 1980s has been largely in new areas, especially in the Asia-Pacific region, and it has regularly resulted in the appropriation and pollution of local waterways to the detriment of local economic practices and the well-being of indigenous communities. Violent protests and 'resource wars' have ensued, with high costs to social stability and well-being.[25]

Controversies over the impacts of mining on water are far from new. Early Japanese scholar Kumazawa Banzan (1619–1691) warned that 'digging mines to export to foreign countries was despoiling Japan's mountains and making its rivers shallow'. What concerned him was not water pollution so much as the apparent shift away from harmony with Nature.[26] In 1877 scientists at Tokyo University reported that, following the careful control of the Tokugawa regime (1600–1867), the purity of Tokyo's water supply surpassed that of Paris and London. But industrialization and international trade meant that mining revenue had begun to exceed that of agriculture.

Barely a decade later, farmers close to the Watarase River just north of Tokyo petitioned for the closure of the Ashio copper mine, because it was polluting the river and had damaged their fields and their health. The water had turned bluish-white, fish had died and anyone who ate them became sick. Fishing communities collapsed when sales were banned. Severe flooding in 1888 and 1890 compounded the problem: crops shrivelled, farm workers developed sores and the villagers pleaded with the national government to close the mine. But copper was Japan's third most important export at the time, and 'caught up in the demands of rapid modernization, Japan's

Kagara Mine at Mount Garnet, Queensland.

153

Mejki government (1868–1912) was not immediately willing to restrict mine activities.'[27]

Contemporary mining technology has made it possible to prevent such extreme water pollution, at least in areas where environmental protection is both demanded and enforced. But there are more insidious pollutants in the run-off from mining and other industries, which affect both fresh and salt waters. Joanna Burger and Michael Gochfeld describe the accumulation of metals such as mercury, cadmium and lead in marine organisms:

> Humans rely heavily on food from the sea, including algae, shellfish; other invertebrates such as crustaceans, octopus and squid; fish, birds and their eggs; and marine mammals . . . Metals exist in solution, bound to particulate matter or incorporated in biota. Once in the water column or sediment, metals can accumulate in organisms.[28]

Chemical solutions

Water quality in many lakes, rivers and oceans is also compromised by the pharmaceutical and cleaning products with which humans sanitize and beautify their bodies and environments: steroids, hormones, antibiotics and anti-inflammatory drugs, as well as detergents, sunscreens, perfumes and veterinary medicines.[29] Via excretion and unchecked by sewage treatment, 'Many are found in high enough concentrations not only to cause harm to aquatic organisms but to pose a potential risk to humans.'[30] Such risks include the effects of 'recycled' contraceptives on fertility; the impacts of steroids and hormones on individual chemical balances; even the risks posed by the use of chlorine to treat drinking water.[31]

As the 'substance of strangers', the polluting fluids of others – like foul flooding – compose the most repugnant category of pollution. No wonder, then, that even as water treatment in many parts of the world has improved in scientific terms, people's anxieties about drinking-water quality have increased rather than decreased. In part, this reflects the more distant social relationships of industrialized societies. Close social connections make sharing water and substance less problematic: consider, for example, how the sharing of bathwater or even a glass of drinking water offers a direct reflection of the levels of intimacy in human relationships. The substance of strangers is a different matter though and, just as personal hygiene and 'containing the self' became more critical with urbanization, so too have ideas about water quality. Most cities now rely on recycled water, and imbibing water that has previously passed through a number of strangers is, at best, considered an unpleasant necessity.

Relationships with water suppliers have also become more distant as these have corporatized. Historically there have been many lively debates about water treatment and the use of chlorine and fluoride, but these doubts have been exacerbated by distrust of the transnational corporations who now own many previously local water supply companies. Similar distrust of industrialized farming and the impact of its activities on waterways adds to these concerns, creating a sense that in making its way through such farmland, and through industrial areas, water quality is further compromised.

So there is an underlying rationale to people's willingness to eschew cheap tap water and pay sometimes a hundred times as much for 'pure' spring water, captured and bottled safely at the source, and so retaining all of the connotations of unspoiled, uncompromised 'living water', 'healing water' and so forth that led, for instance, to Roman notions of 'virgin' streams, and Christian visions of water as the substance of the spirit. Contemporary representations of such products express these generative ideas very clearly – for example, in Evian advertisements in which babies, symbols of new life, gambol underwater, and in Volvic's suggestions that its fizzy mineral water carries vibrant volcanic potency.

It is estimated that within a couple of decades a third of the world's population will be experiencing severe water shortages. Most scientists now agree that climate change will exacerbate these problems, raising temperatures and melting vast glacial water storages. Such effects are evident even in the wettest

Evian babies.

volvic. FILLS YOU WITH VOLCANICITY.

Volvic's volcanic
eruptions of water.

THE DELUGE.

Gustave Doré, *The Deluge*, 1866.

place on Earth, the Amazon, where it used to be said that 'In the dry season it rains every day. In the rainy season it rains all day.' Today, 'things have changed ... Red dust covers Belem ... from the region where there is no rain forest any more, nothing but grass, angry, hungry people, burned tree trunks and white, undernourished cattle.'[32]

Droughts and fluctuations in the waters of the Amazon basin are meaningful – it provides about a fifth of the fresh water that replenishes the earth's oceans. And greater volatility in the movements of water around the world is equally alarming: as well as creating droughts, climate change appears to be increasing the variability of rainfall and bringing more extreme weather events. Societies around the world are now experiencing major floods with increasing frequency.

Katsushika Hokusai, *Under the Wave off Kanagawa*, c. 1831, colour woodblock oban print.

'*Après moi le déluge*'

To be 'swept away', while positive if it carries one into a 'sea of love', more often expresses a loss of control, a whirling away from dry land that threatens the boundaries and the very survival of the self – 'Not waving but drowning'. When Louis XV anticipated the flood of chaos that would overtake French society with the Revolution in the late eighteenth century, his metaphor articulated a terror of being subsumed by water, or events, that all of us can recognize. Even the minor flooding of a home can be deeply disturbing, destroying domestic order, bringing in pollution. But nothing can compare to the fear engendered by major floods that quite literally sweep away everything in their path. When rivers burst their banks, their torrents of water are experienced as traumatic ruptures in the world's proper flow of water.

Such experiences are shared by riverside dwellers in places like New Orleans, Brisbane, Mississippi and other cities devastated

Samoan beachside 'fale'.

by floods in recent years, and by the vast populations of countries such as Bangladesh where these events occur with depressing regularity. There is no doubt that human activities have exacerbated such problems. The draining of riparian and coastal wetlands and the clearance of forests for agriculture have removed the layer of vegetation that used to soak up run-off from hills and mountains. Then there is the impervious concrete covering vast areas, and the 'canalization' of formerly winding rivers. Literally over and above this, of course, is humankind's largest disruption of water, the climate change that leads to more volatile patterns of precipitation, to the major storms that bring torrents downriver, and to the increasing seismic activity that sends tsunami shivers of horror across oceans to low-lying coastal areas made more vulnerable by the removal of the mangrove swamps and marshes that used to diffuse the incoming tide.

An Australian farm after a three-year drought.

The vast waves that arrive as tsunamis take great bites out of people's lives, as if the great maw of hell had broken its bounds and reached onto the safety of land to snatch and swallow all into chaos. People who experience such events lose their faith in the integrity of the shoreline. For example, in Samoa, where a tsunami engulfed a number of villages in 2009, the people who survived remain reluctant to return to their traditional coastal homes.

Disorders in the flow of water around the earth and through social and ecological systems are also manifested in drought. Arid regions have experienced longer and longer droughts, and the temperature rises predicted can only add to the woes of humans and non-humans alike. Like floods, droughts carry massive symbolic weight, being the ultimate expression of a loss of vitality, of generative capacity, of life itself. As desertification spreads, more and more communities are losing their livelihoods and becoming unable to sustain their ways of life. The number of environmental refugees is rising fast and, even now, few countries welcome large migrant influxes and their potentially 'polluting' and destabilizing social and cultural effects. Such reluctance can only increase as water and other resources become the focus of ever more intense competition.

Many environmental refugees are not the victims of direct developmental displacement but represent a starker reality – the fact that ecological systems are simply not infinite in their ability to support rising human populations and intensive processes of production. Nor can they continue to support their non-human inhabitants: loss of habitats and multiple forms of environmental degradation are having a massive impact on biodiversity. There have been several major extinction events previously in earth's history, but we are now contemplating the first caused anthropogenically – by human activities.

According to the IUCN, 'The rapid loss of species we are seeing today is estimated by experts to be between 1,000 and 10,000 times higher than the "background" or expected natural extinction rate.' And this, it adds, 'is a highly conservative estimate'.[33] Quite apart from the moral questions about whether humankind has the right to drive other species to extinction, removing so many participants from such a complex array of interdependent relationships seems unwise. No species – human or otherwise – can avoid the effects of disruption in the orderly flow of water through planetary systems. James Hansen may well be right in predicting 'storms on the horizon'.[34]

Conclusion

Consuming water

The use of water for irrigation, agriculture and industrial power has been central to the exponential growth of human populations. It has been similarly vital in permitting societies to develop economies dependent upon continual growth and expansion in the use of water, land and all other resources. This has been materially beneficial to many, but immensely costly for less powerful people and the non-human beings equally dependent on water. An idea has persisted for many decades that, even if wealth, health and power are unevenly distributed now, eventually, with sufficient technology, environmental damage can be mitigated and all can emulate Western patterns of consumption.

There are many exciting new technologies that enable more efficient water and resource use, and these should be embraced. But the combination of rapid human population growth and almost worldwide aspirations for particular lifestyles raises a major question mark over the capacity of even the most innovative technical advances to achieve long-term human and ecological sustainability. Consider, for a moment, how much water it takes to make things. About ten years ago a British geographer, Anthony Allan, devised a way of calculating how much water is embodied in (used to produce) food and material artefacts.[1] A cup of coffee requires approximately 140 l of 'virtual' water; 500 g of cheese, 2,500 l; 1 kg of rice, 3,400 l; a pair of jeans, 5,400 l; a car, 50,000 l.

As well as becoming 'virtual water' in this way, water used in productive processes also leaves spatially located 'water footprints'

Human population growth.

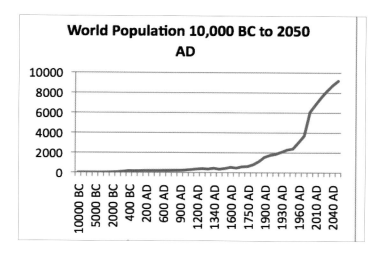

equivalent to the carbon footprints with which we have become familiar.[2] Thus there is a 'bluewater footprint' relating to how much water has been taken from the local environment, and a 'greywater footprint' representing the extent to which that process produces polluted waste water. Based on flows through global supply chains, the distribution of these footprints is wildly unequal: for example, Germany's bluewater footprint extends to over 200 other countries. And while individual Germans use only about 124 l of water a day directly, 'they use a further 5,288 l a day when the water requirements for producing their consumed food, clothes and other daily commodities are included.[3]

This means that about a trillion tonnes of virtual fresh water is traded internationally every year, often from poorer arid regions to wealthier industrial societies in temperate climes.[4] As well as leaving costly water footprints, this water use draws not only on increasingly degraded rivers, but on finite aquifers and the meltwater from shrinking glaciers. Inevitably, it has led to increasing competition for the control of water, and to fierce contests over it.

Transboundary flows

Hydro-squabbles can burst forth with alarming rapidity, and recur whenever people compete to direct the flow of water. Historical

Cubbie Station
diversion channel in
Queensland, Australia.

archives describing the River Stour in Dorset, for example, record
ancient quarrels between water mill owners, with downstream
millers complaining that their upstream neighbours had not ful-
filled agreements about water releases, and were thus depriving
them of their livelihood. *Plus ça change:* to give an Antipodean
example, in a recent case in Queensland, Australia, the argument
(though possibly not the language) could have been lifted from
the Dorset archives. Interstate rivalries in Australia between
Queensland and New South Wales have always been lively,
but have intensified with the construction of a giant private
irrigation scheme at Cubbie Station along the Culgoa River.
The Queensland government gave the station permission to
impound about a quarter of the water that would otherwise flow
across the state boundary into the Darling River, and thus into
one of the world's most degraded river catchment areas, the
Murray Darling Basin. This massive diversion of water to
growing cotton (a highly profitable but immensely thirsty crop)
raised passionate protests from downstream farmers deprived
of their allocations, and from conservationists in despair about
the destruction of some of the Basin's last surviving wetlands,
critical for migratory birds.[5]

Even without interstate rivalries, collaboration is not always
successful, as demonstrated by the bitter 'water wars' in California
which began with conflicts over water in Los Angeles in the late

1800s, and have continued to generate regular battles over water allocations ever since. Even more potentially volatile are the conflicts that arise when nations impound transboundary rivers.

Although collaborating over water management can encourage cooperative relationships across and within national boundaries – as recent efforts to negotiate an agreement to maintain flows in the Colorado River have shown – greater water scarcity makes such positive outcomes more difficult to achieve.[6] The history of water is awash with examples: conflicts between Turkey, Syria and Iraq over the Tigris and Euphrates; over the Nile between Egypt, Ethiopia and the Sudan; and between Israel, Lebanon, Jordan and the Palestinian territories over the River Jordan.

Control over marine resources has long been contentious too. The Cod Wars between Britain and Iceland in the 1950s and '70s revived recently with a quarrel over mackerel. Contests for fishing quotas have regularly soured relationships between Britain and Spain, Australia and Japan, and the USA and Russia. The Aral Sea continues to be a source of tensions between Kazakhstan, Uzbekistan, Turkmenistan, Tajikistan and Kyrgyzstan.

The list of conflicts over water gets even lengthier if it includes the numerous armed conflicts in which access to fresh water, if not the central issue, has been a critical element. There are those who argue that the notion of 'water scarcity' is just a representation intended to facilitate enclosure and control. There may be some truth in this accusation, but even perceptual scarcity has social and political effects – and the evidence suggests that freshwater resources are indeed finite and dwindling. Water shortages readily increase the volatility of political relationships:

> Pakistan . . . is a nuclear-armed state . . . Soon it's going
> to have one third of its water from the Indus River – its
> main water lifeline – dry up from the lost glacier melt. At
> the same time, its population is increasing by 30 percent. So
> in the next 15 years, we can imagine a country that's already
> on the brink, dealing with a loss of 30 percent of its water
> while the population increases by 30 percent. The United

States understands the problem because it agreed in December to pump in $7.5 billion to Pakistan. Half of that is going to water-related projects – storage, irrigation, and hydropower.[7]

Scaremongering is probably unhelpful, but there is clearly a link between unmanageable levels of water deprivation and political instability. UNESCO has suggested that lack of access to water ought to be recognized as a key incentive to terrorism. This elicited a sharp response from Vandana Shiva, who describes terrorists as those

> hiding in corporate boardrooms and behind the free trade rules of the WTO, North American Free Trade Agreement (NAFTA), and Free Trade Area of the Americas (FTAA). They are hiding behind the privatization conditionalities of the IMF and World Bank. By refusing to sign the Kyoto protocol, President Bush is committing an act of ecological terrorism on numerous communities who may very well be wiped off the Earth by global warming. In Seattle, the WTO was dubbed the 'World Terrorist Organization' by protestors because its rules are denying millions the right to a sustainable livelihood.[8]

Implicit in her comments is a central question about who owns water, who shoulders responsibility for its management, and who deals with the social and ecological outcomes of their choices.

Fishing boat in Valdez, Alaska Bay.

Contra flows

In the later twentieth century, intensifying water use, growing awareness that freshwater resources were finite and the rise of neo-liberal commitments to market rule resulted in a rapid privatization of water resources.[9] This was by no means new: attempts had been made to enclose water in various forms of private ownership over the centuries, and these had become more concerted when major infrastructural investments were

needed to modernize water supply systems. But, by and large, commitments to the notion of water as a 'common good', which had prevailed for millennia, held sway, pinned in place partly by democratic ideals which recognized that political enfranchisement and the ownership of key resources were closely linked.

However, in the 1980s, extreme right-wing regimes in both the USA and the UK, keen to devolve governance to the market, gave free rein to neo-liberal ideologies and their practices. In 1989, despite widespread protests, Margaret Thatcher privatized the British water industry, leaving only a weak regulatory body, the Office of Water Services (OFWAT), to protect public interests. A large percentage of the industry was rapidly sold to

Water rights poster,
Mexico City, 2006.

international corporations, water charges rose 60 per cent in
five years and a failure to invest in infrastructure has left the
country subject to lengthy 'droughts' even after months of rain.
The number of water stealers – people tapping illegally into
supply pipes as they did in the Victorian era – is once again on
the rise, in part encouraged by rumbling resentment about the
enclosure of a 'common good'.

Some populations have been less compliant, particularly
when attempts have been made to impose water privatization in
areas where many people already live in extreme poverty. Just
as top-down political power is enabled by the control of water,
counter-movements can also be empowered by refusing to cede
their control of commonly held resources. In 2000, in what became
known as the 'water war', violent public protests successfully
repulsed attempts in Bolivia (made at the behest of the World
Bank) to sell the control of water to an American corporation,
Bechtel, and even to prevent people from collecting rainwater.

Such public outcries have driven privatization underground, to be manifested in 'water-trading' schemes initiated, for example, by John Howard's government in Australia. Though never using the P-word, such schemes effectively privatize water by converting the government's annual water allocations to farmers and industry into private assets that can be traded in a 'virtual' water market. In many cases struggling farmers, unable to compete with the big water buyers such as Cubbie Station, have given up and traded their water allocations away from the land.

With water becoming an increasingly valuable 'asset' in this way, privatization is being pushed by right-wing governments and the transnational water industry. In 2012, for example, Maori groups tried, in vain, to prevent New Zealand's Conservative government from selling off hydro-company shares and their attendant water allocations.

Most often, such shares are bought up by international corporations who neither live in the environments providing the water (or the energy and/or goods produced within it), nor have any interests in common with the people who do. For example, the infamous Cubbie Station was sold, in late 2012, to a Chinese conglomerate. The benefits of the water, like the virtual water in exported goods, are – to use Karl Polanyi's term – 'disembedded'.[10] Rising like steam into the international cash flows of corporate networks, this liquid 'wealth' pools in tax-haven protected reservoirs, while the social and ecological costs are left behind.

For decades now we have heard repetitively (from the beneficiaries) that market rule is preferable to that of government. But competitive regimes produce both winners and losers, and the number of the latter is growing. What is the role of a government? If it devolves water ownership and management to unaccountable elites, is this not an abdication of its most fundamental democratic and moral responsibilities? If the State no longer owns the most vital of resources, who owns the State?

Such questions run like an undercurrent through contemporary discourses about water. The last two decades have brought an increasingly vocal critique of the ecological and social impacts

of dams and development, and the rise of counter-movements opposed to short-term competitive ideologies. One of the outcomes of the water war in Bolivia was to highlight growing alliances between regional counter-movements and global activist networks similarly concerned with democratic rights and the public ownership and control of water.[11] United by simmering discontent with the status quo and a common commitment to principles of equality, these counter-movements are beginning to flow together, pushing the mainstream to take a different, more sustainable direction.

What would a sustainable relationship with water look like? Petri Juuti and his colleagues suggest that 'some of the basic principles of sustainable and viable water governance and services were written more than 2,000 years ago. Using these principles many of the present problems could be avoided and solved.'[12] But, they add, a combination of poor governance, opposition by powerful groups, and the difficulty that we all have in resisting immediate advantages promotes short-term rather than long-term thinking which, as James Hansen points out, leaves 'the storms' to our grandchildren.[13] Is there a way forward that doesn't lead to watery chaos?

Water in utopia

A look at more sustainable lifestyles over time suggests that, while very culturally diverse, in one way or another they have all maintained a series of checks and balances to keep human activities within limits, using resources at a rate matched by the capacities of their material environments to replenish themselves. The reality that there are genuine material constraints to these capacities highlights the internal contradiction in notions of sustainable development. Ivan Illich puts it plainly: '"Sustainable" is the language of balance and limits; "development" is the language of the expectation of more.'[14] Recent economic crises have revived critiques of growth-dependency and constant expansion, promoting the idea of steady state or even 'degrowth' economies. Although contemporary discourses often present them as stand-alone objects, economies do not take place separately from the rest of life: they are simultaneously social and political arrangements and, critically, relationships with our material environments and other species.

So we need to ask what social and material practices enable sustainability – and the answer is probably not untrammelled (and often competitive) population growth. We need to ask what political arrangements produce sustainable resource use and – looking at the current state of affairs – the answer probably doesn't entail leaving people and environments to the mercy of a competitive market. The history of human relationships with water suggests that sustainability relies more on cooperation than competition, and on forms of governance that accommodate the interests of all human and non-human species. If this sounds impossible, we should recall the quotation often attributed to Derek Bok: 'If you think education is expensive, try ignorance.' If you think sustainability is hard to achieve, try living without it.

There have been some nascent efforts to initiate global collaboration on water management: international declarations have upheld human rights to have access to water, and there are calls to extend basic water rights to non-humans.[15] There have been some (rather weak) attempts to devise treaties to tackle climate change issues. The World Water Development report of 2003, while clinging to the mirage of development, acknowledged that the key issue was a need for better governance. There are calls for a worldwide treaty that echoes the principles of the EU Water Directive in articulating the collective responsibilities of all countries in relation to water. Humankind's best hope is that, along with the pressures rising upwards from the 'grass-roots', these top-down efforts will reach a tipping point where they initiate real change.

Sea change

For the first time in human history, it is becoming possible to have global conversations that don't require decades to evolve. The fluidity of communication is now such that ideas whirl around the planet like the *Okeanos* of the ancient Greeks. This opens up new possibilities for human societies to talk to each other about what really matters. But a shift towards more sustainable life-styles needs more than a utilitarian debate over economic policies, or a struggle to solve a practical problem with new technologies and more efficient management. It requires a move away from reductive views of water as merely H_2O, or as just an economic asset. And for this we need our hearts as well as our heads, the arts as well as the sciences.

Many counter-movements have been inspired by passion, not only for social and ecological justice, but for ways of engaging with water that involve the senses and the spirit. A mere consciousness of the pleasures of bathing and drinking water is sufficient to remind us of its centrality in our lives. And the arts and humanities continue to provide avenues to ways of thinking and feeling that are excluded by utilitarian efficiencies. Consider the ways that music evokes what water feels and sounds like,

Marcello Mastroianni
and Anita Ekberg at the
Trevi Fountain in Rome,
from Federico Fellini's
La Dolce Vita, 1960.

what it means. We have 'Old Man River', to remind us how
the inexorable flow of time 'just keeps rolling', and Yiruma's
'The River Flows in You' to celebrate the connections that unite
humans. We have films that use water to speak of effervescent
love, of losses and endings and new beginnings. There is a vast
wealth of imagery in the visual arts that celebrates the meanings
of water: Turner's great seascapes that evoke the ocean's numinous
beauty and its potential chaos, or love scenes focusing on (or in)
fountains and waves.

Every cultural group has its own music and images, its
own ways of reconnecting with water. It is vital that these are
cherished, not forgotten in an unthinking, unfeeling scrabble
for material advantage. Societies need to remember what water
really is, what it means and *why* it matters. Water is the fluid
connection between humankind and every organism on Earth:
we are all the 'hypersea'. The flow of water that animates our own

TITANIC
The World's
Largest Liner
WHITE STAR
LINE
SOUTHAMPTON ~ NEW YORK
VIA CHERBOURG & QUEENSTOWN

Advertisement for the
RMS *Titanic*.

bodies is simultaneously circulating and animating all of the tiny and vast material systems on which we and other species depend. Water is the creative, generative sea that makes and maintains life, and living water is the substance of identity, of the spirit, of the self. We need to replace utilitarian reduction with an appreciation of water as time, memory, movement and flow; as the tides of the heart and the imagination; as the stuff of real 'wealth', which is the combination of health and wholeness. With a sense of fluid belonging, through water, it becomes possible to think and act connectively and collaboratively.

REFERENCES

Introduction

1 Barbara Johnston, Lisa Hiwasaki, Irene Klaver, Amy Ramos-Castillo and Veronica Strang, eds, *Water, Cultural Diversity and Global Environmental Change: Emerging Trends, Sustainable Futures?* (Paris, 2012); Kirsten Hastrup and Frida Hastrup, eds, *Waterworlds: Anthropology in Fluid Environments* (Oxford and New York, 2014); John Wagner, ed., *The Social Life of Water in a Time of Crisis* (Oxford and New York, 2013); Marnie Leybourne and Andrea Gaynor, eds, *Water: Histories, Cultures, Ecologies* (Nedlands, WA, 2006).

1 Water on Earth

1 Lowell's enthusiasm for canal-building Martians may have been misguided, but his endeavours to see into space generated efforts that resulted (fourteen years after his death) in the discovery of Pluto.
2 Personal communication with the author.
3 Humberto Campin and Michael Drake, 'Sources of Terrestrial and Martian Water', in *Water and Life: The Unique Properties of H_2O*, ed. Ruth Lyndon-Bell et al. (Boca Raton, FL, and London, 2010), pp. 221–34.
4 Stefan Helmreich, *Alien Ocean: Anthropological Voyages in Microbial Seas* (Berkeley, CA, 2009).
5 Philip Ball, 'Water as a Biomolecule', in *Water and Life*, ed. Lyndon-Bell et al., p. 49.
6 Poul Astrup et al., *Salt and Water in Culture and Medicine* (Copenhagen, 1993), p. 58.
7 Specific heat is the heat capacity per unit mass of a material.
8 Michael Allaby, *Atmosphere: A Scientific History of Air, Weather and Climate* (New York, 2009).
9 Asit Biswas, *History of Hydrology* (Amsterdam and London, 1970), p. 111.

10 Jianing Chen and Yang Yang, *The World of Chinese Myths* (Beijing, 1995), p. 13; Francis Huxley, *The Dragon: Nature of Spirits, Spirit of Nature* (London, 1979), p. 6.

11 Marek Zvelebil, 'Innovating Hunter-Gatherers: The Mesolithic in the Baltic', in *Mesolithic Europe*, ed. Geoff Bailey and Penny Spikins (Cambridge, 2008), pp. 18–59.

12 Jens Soentgen, 'An Essay on Dew', in *People at the Well: Kinds, Usages and Meanings of Water in a Global Perspective*, ed. Hans Peter Hahn et al. (Frankfurt and New York, 2012), pp. 79–96. Soentgen also notes Cyrano de Bergerac's use of magical dew in efforts to fly to the moon, and the popularity of experiments in which dew was fed into empty eggshells in the hope that this would cause them to fly.

13 Paracelsus observed the greater density or 'heaviness' of salt water, and assumed that this was what was left behind when the lighter fresh water was lifted upwards.

14 Peter Dear, *The Intelligibility of Nature: How Science Makes Sense of the World* (Chicago, IL, 2006).

15 The notion of atoms had been around since being proposed by the Greek philosopher Democritus in about 420 BCE, but Dalton was the first person to provide experimental evidence for the theory.

16 Allaby, *Atmosphere*. Allaby notes that Celsius originally suggested a scale in which 0° was the boiling point and 100° the freezing point, but this was reversed, possibly by his pupil Martin Strömer or by the botanist Carl Linnaeus.

17 Laurent Pfister et al., eds, *Leonardo Da Vinci's Water Theory: On the Origin and Fate of Water* (Wallingford, 2009).

18 Veronica Strang, 'Life Down Under: Water and Identity in an Aboriginal Cultural Landscape', *Goldsmiths College Anthropology Research Papers*, 7 (2002).

19 Andrew Goudie, 'Hydrology', in *The Dictionary of Physical Geography*, ed. David Thomas and Andrew Goudie (Oxford, 2000), pp. 256–7.

20 Jamie Linton, 'Is the Hydrologic Cycle Sustainable? A Historical-Geographical Critique of a Modern Concept', www.sciencevsaging. org, 2 November 2010. These beliefs stemmed in part from ancient Greek ideas about *logos*, the notion that the world was organized according to a defining principle of order, which was interpreted by the Stoics as indicative that there was a divine animating principle. As Thomas McLeish points out, for the ancient Greeks and modern scientists alike, 'The creation of matter itself is not as challenging or as implausible an idea as the creation of *ordered* matter (or alternatively information-containing matter).' Thomas

McLeish, 'Water and Information', in *Water and Life: The Unique Properties of H₂O*, ed. Ruth Lyndon-Bell et al. (Boca Raton, FL, and London, 2010), pp. 203–12.

21 Yi-Fu Tuan, *The Hydrologic Cycle and the Wisdom of God: A Theme in Geoteleology* (Toronto, 1968).

22 Walter Langbein and William Hoyt, *Water Facts for the Nation's Future* (New York, 1959).

23 David Maidment, ed., *Handbook of Hydrology* (New York, 1993), p. 13.

24 Samuel Taylor Coleridge, 'The Rime of the Ancient Mariner', in *Wordsworth and Coleridge: Lyrical Ballads, 1798*, ed. Harold Littledale (London, 1911).

25 Astrup et al., *Salt and Water*, p. 59.

26 Vladimir Vernadsky, *The Biosphere* (Santa Fe, NM, 1986).

27 James Lovelock, *Gaia: A New Look at Life on Earth* (Oxford, 1987). Kepler, like many scientists of the seventeenth century, also subscribed to a view that the movements of the planets and all the material processes on Earth were evidence of God's plan, and were discernible to the 'natural light' of human reason.

28 Lynn Margulis and Mark McMenamin, eds, *Concepts of Symbiogenesis: Historical and Critical Study of the Research of Russian Botanists* (New Haven, CT, 1992); Dianna McMenamin and Mark McMenamin, *Hypersea* (New York, 1994).

2 Living Water

1 This varies with age and health. We do quite literally 'wither' as we age: babies are composed of 75–80 per cent water, and elderly people of 50–60 per cent. Being obese – because fat contains less water – can reduce the percentage to 45 per cent.

2 Joseph Bastien, 'Qollahuaya-Andean Body Concepts: A Topographical-hydraulic Model of Physiology', *American Anthropologist*, LXXXVII/3 (1985), pp. 595–611.

3 Mary Douglas, *Implicit Meanings: Essays in Anthropology* (London, 1975).

4 Patrick L. Barry and Tony Phillip, 'Water on the Space Station', http://spaceflight.nasa.gov, accessed 23 September 2014.

5 Indira Gandhi, *Eternal India* (New Delhi, 1980).

6 Veronica Strang, 'Water and Indigenous Religion: Aboriginal Australia', in *The Idea of Water*, ed. Terje Tvedt and Terje Oestigaard (London, 2009), pp. 343–77.

7 Veronica Strang, 'Representing Water: Visual Anthropology and Divergent Trajectories in Human-environmental Relations', *Anuário Antropológico* (2012), pp. 213–42.

8   Dennis Slifer, *The Serpent and the Sacred Fire: Fertility Images in Southwest Rock Art* (Santa Fe, NM, 2000); Hamilton Tyler, *Pueblo Gods and Myths* (Norman, OK, 1964); Ake Hultkrantz, *Native Religions of North America: The Power of Visions and Fertility* (San Francisco, CA, 1987); Diana Ferguson, *Tales of the Plumed Serpent: Aztec, Inca and Mayan Myths* (London, 2000).

9   Terje Oestigaard, *Water and World Religions: An Introduction* (Bergen, 2005); Sylvie Shaw and Andrew Francis, eds, *Deep Blue: Critical Reflections on Nature, Religion and Water* (London, 2008).

10 This is equally the case with the various kinds of rainbow serpent beings found in Australia and elsewhere, which are often described as Mother Rainbows or Father Rainbows or are seen as containing attributes of both genders.

11 Edward Schafer, *The Divine Woman: Dragon Ladies and Rain Maidens in T'ang Literature* (Berkeley, CA, and London, 1973), p. 14.

12 Norman Austin, *Meaning and Being in Myth* (London, 1989).

13 *Pyramid Texts* no. 1146, cited in Karen Joines, *Serpent Symbolism in the Old Testament: A Linguistic, Archaeological and Literary Study* (New Jersey, 1938), p. 22.

14 Qur'an 31.30.

15 Carol Hillenbrand, 'Gardens Between Which Rivers Flow', in *Rivers of Paradise: Water in Islamic Art and Culture*, ed. Sheila Blair, Sheila and Jonathan Bloom (New Haven, CT, and London, 2009), p. 27.

16 John Day, *God's Conflict with the Dragon and the Sea: Echoes of a Canaanite Myth in the Old Testament* (Cambridge and London, 1985), p. 49.

17 Aboriginal oral histories can have considerable longevity. It has been suggested that the flood stories that are ubiquitous across northern Australia refer to a sea-level rise 10,000 years ago, which pushed many Aboriginal groups inland, and created the Gulf of Carpentaria.

18 Psalms 77:17–21 (et 16–20). See also Psalms 104:26; Job 7:12; Job 38:8; and Jeremiah 5:22, which describe how God shuts in the unruly sea with doors and bars at the time of creation, and places sand as a perpetual barrier. Day, *God's Conflict with the Dragon*, p. 49.

19 Henry Drewal, ed., *Sacred Waters: Arts for Mami Wata and other Water Divinities in Africa and the Diaspora* (Los Angeles, 2008).

20 Mama Zogbé, Chief Hounon-Amengansie, *Mami Wata, Africa's Ancient God/Goddess Revealed: Reclaiming the Ancient History and Sacred Heritage of the Voudoun Religion* (Martinez, GA, n.d.).

21 Claudia Müller-Ebeling, Christian Rätsch and Surendra Shahi, *Shamanism and Tantra in the Himalayas*, trans. Annabel Lee (Rochester, VT, 2002); Omacanda Hāndā, *Naga Cults and Traditions in the Western Himalaya* (New Delhi, 2004).

22 Colin Richards, 'Henges and Water: Towards an Elemental
   Understanding of Monumentality and Landscape in Late
   Neolithic Britain', *Journal of Material Culture*, 1/3 (1996),
   pp. 313–35.
23 Hillenbrand, 'Gardens Between Which Rivers Flow', p. 35.
24 Veronica Strang, *The Meaning of Water* (Oxford and New York,
   2004).
25 Words: Matthias Claudius, 'Wir Pflügen und wir Streuen', in *Paul
   Erdmann's Fest* (1782), trans. Jane Montgomery Campbell (1861);
   music: Johann Schultz (1800).
26 Personal communication with the author.
27 Tim Ingold, 'Earth, Sky, Wind, and Weather', in *Wind, Life,
   Health: Anthropological and Historical Perspectives*, ed. Chris Low
   and Elizabeth Hsu, *Journal of the Royal Anthropological Institute*,
   special issue (2007).
28 Roger Watt, *Understanding Vision* (London, 1991).

3 Imaginary Water

1 Claude Lévi-Strauss, *The Savage Mind* (Chicago, IL, 1966).
2 Mary Douglas, *Natural Symbols* (London, 1973). This work also
   relates to Durkheim's well-known argument that human societies
   use their own political and social arrangements as a mirror in
   defining their religious cosmologies. Voltaire reportedly said
   something similar, commenting that if God had made man in
   His own image, humankind had more than returned the favour;
   Émile Durkheim, *The Elementary Forms of the Religious Life*
   [1912], trans. K. Fields (New York, 1995); Robin Horton and Ruth
   Finnegan, eds, *Modes of Thought: Essays on Thinking in Western and
   Non-Western Societies* (London, 1973); Veronica Strang, 'Familiar
   Forms: Homologues, Culture and Gender in Northern Australia',
   Journal of the Royal Anthropological Society, v/1 (1999), pp. 75–95.
3 Steven Pinker, *How the Mind Works* (London, 1997); George
   Lakoff and Mark Johnson, *Metaphors We Live By* (Chicago, IL,
   1980).
4 Ivan Illich, *H_2O and the Waters of Forgetfulness* (London and New
   York, 1986), p. 24.
5 Veronica Strang, 'Common Senses: Water, Sensory Experience
   and the Generation of Meaning', *Journal of Material Culture*, x/1
   (2005), pp. 93–121.
6 Illich, *H_2O*, pp. 42, 43; Strang, *The Meaning of Water*.
7 Thomas McLeish, 'Water and Information', in *Water and Life: The
   Unique Properties of H_2O*, ed. Ruth Lyndon-Bell et al. (Boca Raton,
   FL, and London, 2010), pp. 203–12.

8 Paul Langley, 'Cause, Condition, Cure: Liquidity in the Global
   Financial Crisis, 2007–8', in *Insights*, III/17 (2010), p. 2.

9 Karl Wittfogel, *Oriental Despotism: A Comparative Study of Total
   Power* (New Haven, CT, 1957).

10 John Donahue and Barbara Johnston, eds, *Water, Culture
   and Power: Local Struggles in a Global Context* (Washington,
   DC, 1998).

11 Franz Krause, 'Rapids on the 'Stream of Life': The Significance of
   Water Movement on the Kemi River', *Worldviews*, special issue,
   XVII/2 (2013), pp. 174–85.

12 John Milton, *Paradise Lost* (London, 1795).

13 J. Ross Goforth (music and lyrics), 'Lethe's Water', in *A Ghost
   Considers Euchre*, released 2 June 2010.

14 Joan Metge, *The Maoris of New Zealand* (London, 1967), p. 37.

15 Jane Hirschfield, trans., 'Uvavnuk', untitled shaman song, in *Women
   in Praise of the Sacred* (New York, 1994).

16 Rodney Giblett, *Postmodern Wetlands: Culture, History, Ecology*
   (Edinburgh, 1996), p. xi.

17 John Bunyan, *Pilgrim's Progress From This World to That Which is to
   Come* (London, 1678).

18 J. G. Ballard, *The Drowned World* [1962] (New York, 2012).

19 Sigmund Freud, *New Introductory Lectures on Psycho-analysis,
   Lecture XXXI*, standard edition, XXII (London, 1964), p. 73.

20 David Gilmore, *Monsters: Evil Beings, Mythical Beasts, and All
   Manner of Imaginary Terrors* (Philadelphia, PA, 2003), pp. 1, 16.

21 Stevie Smith, 'Not Waving But Drowning', in *Collected Poems*
   [1957] (New York, 1983), pp. 393–6.

22 William Wordsworth, 'Sonnet on Seeing Miss Helen Maria
   Williams Weep at a Tale of Distress,' in *The Poetical Works* [1787]
   (Chicago, IL, 1916).

4 Water Journeys

1 Stephen Oppenheimer, *Out of Africa's Eden: The Peopling of the
   World* (Johannesburg, 2003), www.bradshawfoundation.com/journey,
   accessed 29 September 2014.

2 Émile Durkheim, *The Elementary Forms of the Religious Life*, trans.
   K. Fields (New York, 1995)

3 Gaston Bachelard, *Water and Dreams: An Essay on the Imagination
   of Matter*, trans., Edith Farrell (Dallas, TX, 1983).

4 Anne Solomon, 'The Myth of Ritual Origins? Ethnography,
   Mythology and Interpretation of San Rock Art', in *South African
   Archaeological Bulletin* (1997), www.antiquityofman.com, accessed
   29 September 2014.

5   George Silberbauer, *Hunter and Habitat in the Central Kalahari Desert* (Cambridge, 1981), p. 113.

6   A. Whyte et al., 'Human Evolution in Polynesia', in *Human Biology*, 77 (2005), pp. 157–77.

7   P. Sheppard et al., *Lapita: Ancestors and Descendants* (Auckland, 2009).

8   Although it is commonly assumed that land clearance came with European settlement, approximately 46 per cent of New Zealand's forests had been cleared for horticulture prior to the arrival of the British.

9   Jared Diamond, 'The Worst Mistake in the History of the Human Race', *Discover Magazine*, p. 64.

10 Jan Christie, 'Water and Rice in Early Java and Bali', in *A World of Water: Rain, Rivers and Seas in Southeast Asian Histories*, ed. Peter Boomgaard, (Leiden, 2007), p. 235.

11 Karl Butzer, *Early Hydraulic Civilisation in Egypt: A Study in Cultural Ecology* (Chicago, IL, and London, 1976), p. 19.

12 William Albright, *From the Stone Age to Christianity: Monotheism and the Historical Process* (Baltimore, MD, 1946).

13 Ibid., p. 134.

14 Elliot Smith, *The Evolution of the Dragon* (London, New York and Manchester, 1919), p. 29.

15 Isaiah 48:1, Numbers 24:7.

16 Qur'an 36. 6.

17 Francis Huxley, *The Dragon: Nature of Spirit, Spirit of Nature* (London, 1979), p. 8.

18 Ibid., p. 9.

19 Marinus de Visser, *The Dragon in China and Japan* (Wiesbaden, 1969), p. 38.

20 Edward Schafer, *The Divine Woman: Dragon Ladies and Rain Maidens in T'ang Literature* (Berkeley, CA, and London, 1973).

21 Aylward Blackman, 'The Significance of Incense and Libations in Funerary and Temple Ritual', in *Zeitschrift für Ägyptische Sprache und Altertumskunde*, 50 (Leipzig, 1912), p. 69.

22 Butzer, *Early Hydraulic Civilisation in Egypt.*

23 Smith, *The Evolution of the Dragon*, p. viii.

24 Asit Biswas, *History of Hydrology* (Amsterdam and London, 1970), pp. 2–3.

25 Florence Padovani, 'The Chinese Way of Harnessing Rivers: the Yangtze River', in *A History of Water* 1: *Water Control and River Biographies*, ed. Terje Tvedt and Eva Jakobsson (London, 2006), pp. 12–43.

26 John Pierpont, 'Deploring the Reign of Intemperance', in *Cold Water Melodies, and Washingtonian Songster* (Boston, MA, 1842).

27 Bernard Batto, *Slaying the Dragon: Mythmaking in the Biblical Tradition* (Louisville, KT, 1992), p. 48.

28 Samantha Riches, *St George: Hero, Martyr and Myth* (Stroud, 2000).

29 Anton Szandor LaVey, *The Satanic Bible* (New York, 1969).

5 Redirections

1 Veronica Strang, *Gardening the World: Agency, Identity and the Ownership of Water* (Oxford and New York, 2009); Veronica Strang, 'Going Against the Flow: The Biopolitics of Dams and Diversions', *Worldviews*, special issue, XVII/2 (2013), pp. 161–73.

2 Water also provided protective moats and routes for invasion or escape. For example, in about 1200 BCE 'sinnors', or water tunnels, provided secret ways out of cities such as Jerusalem. *The Second Book of Chronicles* notes how King Hezekiah constructed one, 'to the east side of the city of David', cited in Asit Biswas, *History of Hydrology* (Amsterdam and London, 1970), p. 22.

3 George Smith, *History of Sennacherib* (London, 1878).

4 Cuneiform tablet translation from *Bellino Cylinder*, lines 39–42, in Smith, *History of Sennacherib*, p. 142.

5 From the *Bavian Inscription*, lines 6–17, in Smith, *History of Sennacherib*, pp. 157–60.

6 The Great Bath at Mohenjodaro has been described as the earliest public water tank of the ancient world. Two staircases lead into the large mud-brick structure lined with bitumen, which may have been used for ritual bathing or religious ceremonies.

7 Larry Mays, *Ancient Water Technologies* (Dordrecht, 2010).

8 Qur'an, 34. 14.

9 Sextus Julius Frontinus, *Frontinus: The Stratagems and The Aqueducts of Rome*, trans. Charles Bennett (London and New York, 1975).

10 Mark Busse and Veronica Strang, *Ownership and Appropriation* (Oxford and New York, 2010).

11 Hazel Dodge, 'Greater than the Pyramids': The Water Supply of Ancient Rome', in *Ancient Rome: The Archaeology of the Eternal City*, ed. J. C. Coulston and Heather Dodge (Oxford, 2000), p. 166.

12 Jamie Linton, *What is Water?: The History of a Modern Abstraction* (Vancouver, 2010).

13 Robert Friedel, *A Culture of Improvement* (Cambridge, MA, and London, 2007).

14 Heather Sutherland, 'Geography as Destiny? The Role of Water in Southeast Asian History', in *A World of Water: Rain, Rivers and Seas*

in Southeast Asian Histories, ed. Peter Boomgaard (Leiden, 2007), pp. 27–70.

15 Kenneth Hall, 'Economic History of Southeast Asia', in *The Cambridge History of Southeast Asia: From Early Times to ca. 1500*, ed. Nicholas Tarling (Cambridge, 1999), pp. 185–275.

16 Terje Oestigaard, 'The Topography of Holy Water in England after the Reformation', in *Perceptions of Water in Britain from Early Modern Times to the Present: An Introduction*, ed. Karen Lykke Syse and Terje Oestigaard (Bergen, 2010), p. 24.

17 Samuel Baker, *Written on the Water: British Romanticism and the Maritime Empire of Culture* (Charlottesville, VA, 2010), p. 1.

18 Olaus Magnus, *History of the Northern Peoples* (Rome, 1555).

19 Herman Melville, *Moby-Dick; or, The Whale* (New York, 1851).

20 Witi Ihimaera, *Whale Rider* (London, 2005); Film of the same name dir. Niki Caro (2002).

6 The Power of Industry

1 David Pietz, 'Controlling the Waters in Twentieth-century China: The Nationalist State and the Huai River', in *A History of Water* 1: *Water Control and River Biographies*, ed. Terje Tvedt and Eva Jakobsson (London, 2006), pp. 92–119.

2 Ibid. p. 93.

3 Ahmed Kamal, 'Living with Water: Bangladesh since Ancient Times', in *A History of Water*, ed. Tvedt and Jakobsson, p. 197.

4 Roberta Magnusson, 'Water and Wastes in Medieval London', in *A History of Water*, ed. Tvedt and Jakobsson, pp. 299–313.

5 Dolly Jorgenson, 'What to Do with Waste', in *Living Cities: An Anthology in Urban Environmental History*, ed. Sven Lilja and Mattias Legner (Stockholm, 2012), p. 46.

6 Majorie Honeybourne, 'The Fleet and its Neighborhood in Early and Medieval Times', in *Transactions of the London and Middlesex Archaeological Society*, XIX (1947), pp. 51–2.

7 Ideas about water treatment had been around for a long time: ancient Greek, Sanskrit and Egyptian records describe ways of filtering water through sand, charcoal and ash to trap sediments and decrease turbidity, but little was done in this regard in London until the early 1800s.

8 The watering of riparian meadows prevented them from freezing, and so lengthened the period during which grass would grow.

9 Terje Tvedt and Eva Jakobsson, 'Introduction', in *A History of Water*, ed. Tvedt and Jakobsson, p. xi.

10 Richard White, *The Organic Machine: The Remaking of the Columbia River* (New York, 1995), p. 3.

11 Ibid., p. 30.

12 Ivan Illich, 'The Shadow Our Future Throws', *New Perspectives Quarterly*, XVI/2 (1999), p. 18.

13 Pierre Bourdieu, *Distinction: A Social Critique of the Judgement of Taste*, trans. Richard Nice (London, 2010).

14 Jean-Pierre Goubert, *The Conquest of Water: The Advent of Health in the Industrial Age*, trans. Andrew Wilson (Princeton, NJ, 1986), p. 241.

15 Hugh Barty-King, *Water – The Book: An Illustrated History of Water Supply and Wastewater in the United Kingdom* (London, 1992), p. 135.

16 Ivan Illich, *H2O and the Waters of Forgetfulness* (London and New York, 1986), p. 1.

17 Ibid., p. 3.

18 Hippocrates (464–372 BCE) had used baths to cure disease and even built a health resort, Asclepeion, on the island of Kos. The Romans also had a keen interest in balneo-therapy, and spread these ideas and practices across Europe.

19 Poul Astrup, Peter Bie and Hans Engell, *Salt and Water in Culture and Medicine* (Copenhagen, 1993).

20 Susan Anderson, 'The Pleasure of Taking the Waters', in *Water, Leisure and Culture: European Historical Perspectives*, ed. Susan Anderson and Bruce Tabb (Oxford and New York, 2002), pp. 1–2.

21 Karen Lykke Syse, 'Ideas of Leisure, Pleasure and the River in Early Modern England', in *Perceptions of Water in Britain from Early Modern Times to the Present: An Introduction*, ed. Karen Lykke Syse and Terje Oestigaard (Bergen, 2010), p. 36.

22 Veronica Strang, 'Sustaining Tourism in Far North Queensland', in *People and Tourism in Fragile Environments*, ed. Martin Price (London, 1996), pp. 51–67.

7 Engineering Utopia

1 Yves-Marie Allain and Janine Christiany, *L'Art des Jardins en Europe* (Paris, 2006).

2 Marilyn Symmes, *Fountains, Splash and Spectacle: Water and Design from the Renaissance to the Present* (London, 1998).

3 Toru Dutt, 'Le Fond de la mer', in *A Sheaf Gleaned in French Fields*, 3rd edn (1880).

4 In fact the Stour begins a little further uphill, in a number of springs around St Peter's Pump, but these are gathered into a single stream, which is directed into the pool.

5 Ivan Illich, 'The Shadow Our Future Throws', *New Perspectives Quarterly*, XVI/2 (1999).

6 Edward Said, *Culture and Imperialism* (New York, 1993), p. 271.

7 Donald Worster, 'Water in the Age of Imperialism and Beyond', in *A History of Water* 3: *A World of Water*, ed. Terje Tvedt and Terje Oestigaard (London, 2006), pp. 5–17; Yi-Fu Tuan, *The Hydrologic Cycle and the Wisdom of God: A Theme in Geoteleology* (Toronto, 1968).

8 Marc Reisner, *Cadillac Desert: The American West and its Disappearing Water* (London, 2001); Donald Worster, *Rivers of Empire: Water, Aridity and the Growth of the American West* (Oxford and New York, 1992).

9 Ernestine Hill, *Water into Gold: The Taming of the Mighty Murray River* [1937] (London and Sydney, 1965), p. v.

10 Jamie Linton, *What is Water?: The History of a Modern Abstraction* (Vancouver, 2010), p. 83.

11 Mattias Tagseth, 'The Mfongo Irrigation Systems on the Slopes of Mt Kilimanjaro, Tanzania', in *A History of Water* 1: *Water Control and River Biographies*, ed. Terje Tvedt and Eva Jakobsson (London, 2006), p. 489.

12 Ibid., p. 493.

13 Ibid., p. 489.

14 Jamie Linton, 'Is the Hydrologic Cycle Sustainable? A Historical-Geographical Critique of a Modern Concept', www.sciencevsaging. org, 2 November 2010.

15 The Hoover Dam was built between 1931 and 1936.

16 David Pietz, 'Controlling the Waters in Twentieth-century China', in *A History of Water* 1: *Water Control and River Biographies*, ed. T. Tvedt and Eva Jakobsson (London, 2006), pp. 92–119.

17 Bettina Weiz, 'Water Makes the Difference: The Case of South India', in *People at the Well: Kinds, Usages and Meanings of Water in a Global Perspective*, ed. Hans Peter Hahn et al. (Frankfurt and New York 2012), pp. 190–216.

18 Roger Deakin, *Waterlog: A Swimmer's Journey Through Britain* (London, 2000).

19 Kenneth Grahame, *The Wind in the Willows* (London, 1908). Here, Ratty is speaking to Mole.

20 David Reason, 'Reflections of Wilderness and Pike Lake Pond', in *Personal, Societal, and Ecological Values of Wilderness: Congress and Proceedings on Research, Management, and Allocation*, 1. Forest Service Proceedings (Fort Collins, co, 1998), p. 86.

21 Kay Milton, ed., *Environmentalism: The View from Anthropology* (London, 1993).

22 Maria Cruz-Torres, *Lives of Dust and Water: An Anthropology of Change and Resistance in Northwestern Mexico* (Tucson, az, 2004); Benjamin Orlove, *Lines in the Water: Nature and Culture at Lake Titicaca* (Berkeley, ca, 2002).

8 **Water Pressures**

1 Jacques Leslie, *Deep Water: The Struggle Over Dams, Displaced People and the Environment* (London, 2006).

2 Benjamin Chao, 'Anthropogenic Impact on Global Geodynamics Due to Water Impoundment in Major Reservoirs', *Geophysical Research*, 22 (1995), pp. 3533–6.

3 Michael Cernea, 'Risks, Safeguards, and Reconstruction: A Model for Population Dis-placement and Resettlement', in *Applied Anthropology: Domains of Application*, ed. Satish Kedia and John van Willigen (Westport, CT, 2000), p. 19.

4 Yan Tan et al., 'Rural Women, Displacement and the Three Gorges Project', *Development and Change*, XXXVI/4 (2001), pp. 711–34.

5 'The World Commission on Dams', www.internationalrivers.org, accessed 4 February 2012.

6 Ibid.

7 Gerardo Halsema and Linden Vincent, 'Of Flumes, Modules and Barrels: The Failure of Irrigation Institutions and Technologies to Achieve Equitable Water Control in the Indus Basin', in *A History of Water* 1: *Water Control and River Biographies*, ed. Terje Tvedt and Eva Jakobsson (London, 2006), pp. 55–91.

8 Stephen Lansing, *Priests and Programmers: Technologies of Power in the Engineered Landscape of Bali* (Princeton, NJ, and Oxford, 1991).

9 Sanjeev Khagram, *Dams and Development: Transnational Struggles for Water and Power* (Ithaca, NY, 2004).

10 Friends of River Narmada, 'A Brief Introduction to the Narmada Issue', www.narmada.org/introduction.html, accessed 29 September 2014.

11 Arundhati Roy, *The Cost of Living* (New York, 2007).

12 Robert Foster, 'The Work of the New Economy: Consumers, Brands, and Value Creation', *Cultural Anthropology*, XXII/4 (2007), pp. 707–73. See also www.righttowater.info.

13 Jun Jing, 'Villages Dammed, Villages Repossessed: A Memorial Movement in Northwest China', *American Ethnologist*, XXVI/2 (1999), pp. 324–43.

14 Petri Juuti, Tapio Katko and Heikki Vuorinen, eds, *Environmental History of Water: Global View of Community Water Supply and Sanitation* (London, 2007).

15 Julian Caldecott, *Water: The Causes, Costs and Future of a Global Crisis* (London, 2008).

16 Natural Heritage Trust, *Dryland Salinity in Australia: A Summary of the National Land and Water Resources Audit's Australian Dryland Salinity Assessment* (Canberra, 2001), p. 3. See http://lwa.gov.au, accessed 29 September 2014.

17 In 2012, the Environmental Defense Fund persuaded the u.s. and Mexico to sign a bi-national agreement to work together to restore the Colorado River and ensure that regular flows of water reached the wetlands at its estuaries; see Marc Reisner, *Cadillac Desert: The American West and its Disappearing Water* (London, 2001).

18 Scientists, including a 2011 IUCN task force, have highlighted the impacts of neonicotinoids on bee populations. This is not merely a threat to bees themselves: globally, bees pollinate about three-quarters of the world's food crops – about a third of the food on which humans depend.

19 'Nearly 200,000 tons of agricultural pesticides are used annually within the European Union'. Simon Meissner, 'Virtual Water and Water Footprints', in *People at the Well: Kinds, Usages and Meanings of Water in a Global Perspective*, ed. Hans Peter Hahn et al. (Frankfurt, 2012), pp. 44–64 (p. 59).

20 International Union for the Conservation of Nature, 'Species Extinction – The Facts', http://cmsdata.iucn.org/downloads/species_extinction_05_2007.pdf, accessed 29 September 2014.

21 Ibid.

22 Kimberley Patton, *The Sea Can Wash Away All Evils: Modern Marine Pollution and the Ancient Cathartic Ocean* (New York, 2007).

23 Shirley Roburn, 'Sounding a Sea-change: Acoustic Ecology and Arctic Ocean Governance', in *Thinking With Water*, ed. Celia Chen, Janine Macleod and Astrida Neimanis (Montreal, 2013), pp. 106–28.

24 Stuart Kirsch, 'Mining and Environmental Human Rights in Papua New Guinea', in *Transnational Corporations and Human Rights*, ed. Jedrzej Frynas and Scott Pegg (Houndmills and New York, 2003), pp. 115–36.

25 Chris Ballard and Glenn Banks, 'Resource Wars: The Anthropology of Mining', *Annual Review of Anthropology*, XXXII (2003), pp. 287–313.

26 Patricial Sippel, 'Keeping Running Water Clean: Mining and Pollution in Pre-industrial Japan', in *A History of Water*, ed. Tvedt and Jakobsson, p. 427.

27 Ibid., p. 419.

28 Joanna Burger and Michael Gochfeld, 'Metals: Ocean Ecosystems and Human Health', in *Oceans and Human Health: Risks and Remedies from the Seas*, ed. Patrick Walsh et al. (London, 2008), p. 145.

29 'In Germany, more than 30,000 tons of medicinal products are consumed annually distributed over more than 3,000 active ingredients . . . more than 100 different pharmaceutical substances have been detected in water bodies so far'; Meissner, 'Virtual Water and Water Footprints', p. 59.

30 Danielle McDonald and Daniel Riemer, 'The Fate of
    Pharmaceuticals and Personal Care Products in the Environment',
    in *Oceans and Human Health*, pp. 161–79.
31 Per Magnus, Jouni Jaakkola, Anders Skrondal, Jan Alexander,
    Georg Becher, Truls Krogh and Erik Dybing, 'Water Chlorination
    and Birth Defects', *Epidemiology*, x/5 (1999), pp. 513–17.
32 Hilbert, Klaus, 'Water in Amazonia', in *People at the Well: Kinds,
    Usages and Meanings of Water in a Global Perspective*, ed. Hans Peter
    Hahn, Karlheinz Cless and Jens Soentgen (Frankfurt and New
    York, 2012), pp. 236, 243.
33 International Union for the Conservation of Nature, 'Species
    Extinction – The Facts'.
34 James Hansen, *Storms of My Grandchildren* (New York, 2009).

Conclusion

 1 Anthony Allan, *Virtual Water: Tackling the Threat to Our Planet's
    Most Precious Resource* (London, 2011).
 2 Simon Meissner, 'Virtual Water and Water Footprints', in
    *People at the Well: Kinds, Usages and Meanings of Water in a Global
    Perspective*, ed. Hans Peter Hahn et al. (Frankfurt, 2012),
    pp. 44–64.
 3 Ibid., p. 54.
 4 Julian Caldecott, *Water: The Causes, Costs and Future of a Global
    Crisis* (London, 2008).
 5 Veronica Strang, 'Dam Nation: Cubbie Station and the Waters of
    the Darling', in *The Social Life of Water in a Time of Crisis*, ed. John
    Wagner (Oxford and New York, 2013), pp. 36–60.
 6 Ines Dombrowsky, *Conflict, Cooperation and Institutions in
    International Water Management: An Economic Analysis*
    Cheltenham and Northampton, MA, 2007).
 7 Stephen Solomon, *Water: The Epic Struggle for Wealth, Power,
    and Civilization* (New York, 2010).
 8 Vandana Shiva, *Water Wars: Pollution, Profit and Privatization*
    (Cambridge, MA, 2002), p. xiv.
 9 Karen Bakker, *An Uncooperative Commodity: Privatising Water in
    England and Wales* (Oxford, 2003).
10 Karl Polanyi, *The Great Transformation* (New York, 1975).
11 Robert Albro, '"The Water is Ours, Carajo!": Deep Citizenship
    in Bolivia's Water War', in *Social Movements: An Anthropological
    Reader*, ed. June Nash (London, 2005), pp. 249–68.
12 Petri Juuti, Tapio Katko and Heikki Vuorinen, eds, *Environmental
    History of Water: Global View of Community Water Supply and
    Sanitation* (London, 2007).

13 James Hansen, *Storms of My Grandchildren* (New York, 2009).
14 Ivan Illich, 'The Shadow Our Future Throws', *New Perspectives Quarterly*, XVI/2 (1999).
15 The UN Resolution 64/292 (2010) recognized human rights to water and sanitation.

SELECT BIBLIOGRAPHY

Allaby, Michael, *Atmosphere: A Scientific History of Air, Weather and Climate* (New York, 2009)

Anderson, Susan and Bruce Tabb, eds, *Water, Leisure and Culture: European Historical Perspectives* (Oxford and New York, 2002)

Astrup, Poul, Peter Bie and Hans Engell, *Salt and Water in Culture and Medicine* (Copenhagen, 1993)

Austin, Norman, *Meaning and Being in Myth* (London, 1989)

Bachelard, Gaston, *Water and Dreams: An Essay on the Imagination of Matter*, trans. Edith Farrell (Dallas, TX, 1983)

Baker, Samuel, *Written on the Water: British Romanticism and the Maritime Empire of Culture* (Charlottesville, VA, 2010)

Bakker, Karen, *An Uncooperative Commodity: Privatising Water in England and Wales* (Oxford, 2003)

Ballard, J. G., *The Drowned World* [1962] (New York, 2012)

Barty-King, Hugh, *Water – The Book: An Illustrated History of Water Supply and Wastewater in the United Kingdom* (London, 1992)

Biswas, Asit, *History of Hydrology* (Amsterdam and London, 1970)

Boomgaard, Peter, ed., *A World of Water: Rain, Rivers and Seas in Southeast Asian Histories* (Leiden, 2007)

Busse, Mark and Veronica Strang, eds, *Ownership and Appropriation* (Oxford and New York, 2010)

Butzer, Karl, *Early Hydraulic Civilisation in Egypt: A Study in Cultural Ecology* (Chicago, IL, and London, 1976)

Caldecott, Julian, *Water: The Causes, Costs and Future of a Global Crisis* (London, 2008)

Chen, Celia, Janine Macleod and Astrida Neimanis, eds, *Thinking with Water* (Montreal, 2013)

Chen, Jianing, and Yang Yang, *The World of Chinese Myths* (Beijing, 1995)

Cruz-Torres, Maria, *Lives of Dust and Water: An Anthropology of Change and Resistance in Northwestern Mexico* (Tucson, AZ, 2004)

Deakin, Roger, *Waterlog: A Swimmer's Journey Through Britain* (London, 2000)

Dear, Peter, *The Intelligibility of Nature: How Science Makes Sense of the World* (Chicago, IL, 2006)

Donahue, John and Barbara Johnston, eds, *Water, Culture and Power: Local Struggles in a Global Context* (Washington, DC, 1998)

Douglas, Mary, *Implicit Meanings: Essays in Anthropology* (London, 1975)

Ferguson, Diana, *Tales of the Plumed Serpent: Aztec, Inca and Mayan Myths* (London, 2000)

Giblett, Rodney, *Postmodern Wetlands: Culture, History, Ecology* (Edinburgh, 1996)

Goubert, Jean-Pierre, *The Conquest of Water: The Advent of Health in the Industrial Age*, trans. Andrew Wilson (Princeton, NJ, 1986)

Hahn, Hans Peter, Karlheinz Cless and Jens Soentgen, eds, *People at the Well: Kinds, Usages and Meanings of Water in a Global Perspective* (Frankfurt and New York, 2012)

Hastrup, Kirsten, and Frida Hastrup, eds, *Waterworlds: Anthropology in Fluid Environments* (Oxford and New York, 2014)

Helmreich, Stefan, *Alien Ocean: Anthropological Voyages in Microbial Seas* (Berkeley, CA, 2009)

Hill, Ernestine, *Water into Gold: The Taming of the Mighty Murray River* [1937] (London and Sydney, 1965)

Huxley, Francis, *The Dragon: Nature of Spirit, Spirit of Nature* (London, 1979)

Illich, Ivan, *H2O and the Waters of Forgetfulness* (London and New York, 1986)

—, 'The Shadow Our Future Throws', *New Perspectives Quarterly*, XVI/2 (1999), pp. 14–18

Johnston, Barbara, Lisa Hiwasaki, Irene Klaver, Amy Ramos-Castillo and Veronica Strang, eds, *Water, Cultural Diversity and Global Environmental Change: Emerging Trends, Sustainable Futures?* (Paris, 2012)

Juuti, Petri, Tapio Katko and Heikki Vuorinen, eds, *Environmental History of Water: Global View of Community Water Supply and Sanitation* (London, 2007)

Khagram, Sanjeev, *Dams and Development: Transnational Struggles for Water and Power* (Ithaca, NY, 2004)

Krause, Franz, and Veronica Strang, eds, 'Living Water: The Powers and Politics of a Vital Substance', *Worldviews*, special issue, XVII/2 (2013)

Lakoff, George, and Mark Johnson, *Metaphors We Live By* (Chicago, IL, 1980)

Lansing, Stephen, *Priests and Programmers: Technologies of Power in the Engineered Landscape of Bali* (Princeton, NJ, and Oxford, 1991)

Leslie, Jacques, *Deep Water: The Struggle Over Dams, Displaced People and the Environment* (London, 2006)

Leybourne, Marnie and Andrea Gaynor, eds, *Water: Histories, Cultures, Ecologies* (Nedlands, WA, 2006)

Linton, Jamie, *What is Water?: The History of a Modern Abstraction* (Vancouver, 2010)

Lovelock, James, *Gaia: A New Look at Life on Earth* (Oxford, 1987)

Lykke Syse, Karen, and Terje Oestigaard, eds, *Perceptions of Water in Britain from Early Modern Times to the Present: An Introduction* (Bergen, 2010)

Lyndon-Bell, Ruth, et al., eds, *Water and Life: The Unique Properties of H_2O* (Boca Raton, FL, and London, 2010)

McMenamin, Dianna, and Mark McMenamin, *Hypersea* (New York, 1994)

Maidment, David, ed., *Handbook of Hydrology* (New York, 1993)

Margulis, Lynn, and Mark McMenamin, eds, *Concepts of Symbiogenesis: Historical and Critical Study of the Research of Russian Botanists* (New Haven, CT, 1992)

Mays, Larry, *Ancient Water Technologies* (Dordrecht, 2010)

Oestigaard, Terje, *Water and World Religions: An Introduction* (Bergen, 2005)

Oppenheimer, Stephen, *Out of Africa's Eden: The Peopling of the World* (Johannesburg, 2003)

Orlove, Benjamin, *Lines in the Water: Nature and Culture at Lake Titicaca* (Berkeley, CA, 2002)

Patton, Kimberley, *The Sea Can Wash Away All Evils: Modern Marine Pollution and the Ancient Cathartic Ocean* (New York, 2007)

Pfister, Laurent, Hubert Savenije and Fabrizio Fenicia, *Leonardo Da Vinci's Water Theory: On the Origin and Fate of Water* (Wallingford, 2009)

Pinker, Steven, *How the Mind Works* (London, 1997)

Reisner, Marc, *Cadillac Desert: The American West and its Disappearing Water* (London, 2001)

Schafer, Edward, *The Divine Woman: Dragon Ladies and Rain Maidens in T'ang Literature* (Berkeley, CA, and London, 1973)

Shaw, Sylvie and Andrew Francis, eds, *Deep Blue: Critical Reflections on Nature, Religion and Water* (London, 2008)

Solomon, Stephen, *Water: The Epic Struggle for Wealth, Power, and Civilization* (New York, 2010)

Strang, Veronica, 'Life Down Under: Water and Identity in an Aboriginal Cultural Landscape', in *Goldsmiths College Anthropology Research Papers*, 7 (2002)

—, *The Meaning of Water* (Oxford and New York, 2004)

—, *Gardening the World: Agency, Identity and the Ownership of Water* (Oxford and New York, 2009)

Symmes, Marilyn, *Fountains, Splash and Spectacle: Water and Design from the Renaissance to the Present* (London, 1998)

Tuan, Yi-Fu, *The Hydrologic Cycle and the Wisdom of God: A Theme in Geoteleology* (Toronto, 1968)

Tvedt, Terje and Eva Jakobsson, eds, *A History of Water 1: Water Control and River Biographies* (London, 2006)

—, and Terje Oestigaard, eds, *The Idea of Water* (London, 2009)

Vernadsky, Vladimir, *The Biosphere* (Santa Fe, NM, 1986)

Wagner, John, ed., *The Social Life of Water in a Time of Crisis* (Oxford and New York, 2013)

Walsh, Patrick, Sharon Smith, Lora Fleming, Helena Solo-Gabriele and William Gerwick, eds, *Oceans and Human Health: Risks and Remedies from the Seas* (London, 2008)

White, Richard, *The Organic Machine: The Remaking of the Columbia River* (New York, 1995)

Wittfogel, Karl, *Oriental Despotism: A Comparative Study of Total Power* (New Haven, CT, 1957)

ASSOCIATIONS AND WEBSITES

Care International, Water
www.careinternational.org.uk/what-we-do/water-and-sanitation

Conservation International
www.conservation.org

European Centre for River Restoration
www.restorerivers.eu

Global Water
http://globalwater.org

Grassroots International
www.grassrootsonline.org/news/blog/water-rights-whats-wrong?

Greenpeace International
www.greenpeace.org/international/en

International Network of Basin Organizations
www.inbo-news.org

International Panel on Climate Change
www.ipcc.ch

International Programme on the State of the Ocean
www.stateoftheocean.org

International Union for Conservation of Nature
www.iucn.org

International Water Association
www.iwahq.org

International Water History Association
www.iwha.net

The Rivers Trust
www.theriverstrust.org

United Nations, International Decade for Action 'Water for Life' 2005–15
www.un.org/waterforlifedecade

United Nations, Resolution 64/292 (the human right to water and sanitation)
www.un.org/waterforlifedecade

WaterAid
www.wateraid.org/uk

The Water Project
http://thewaterproject.org

World Health Organization, Water and Sanitation
www.who.int/water_sanitation_health/en

ACKNOWLEDGEMENTS

I would like to thank the Institute of Advanced Study (IAS) at Durham University for the *Water* Fellowship in 2009 that allowed me to broaden my research and engage with multiple disciplinary perspectives. This was such an enlightening experience that I have since taken up a full-time post at the Institute. The book has benefited from the advice of colleagues across the discipinary spectrum, including astrophysicist Martin Ward; archaeologist Tony Wilkinson; science writer Philip Ball; medieval historian Giles Gasper; classicist Barbara Graziosi; physicist Tom Mcleish; theologian David Wilkinson; anthropologist Tom Csordas and others. I would also like to thank the friends in Oxford who fed and housed me while I dived into the water literature in the Bodleian Library. And I am grateful to the many colleagues and informants in Malawi, Vietnam, China, New Zealand, Australia and other far-flung parts of the globe, who have provided a veritable wellspring of water stories.

Permissions

PHOTO ACKNOWLEDGEMENTS

The author and the publishers wish to express their thanks to the below sources of illustrative material and /or permission to reproduce it.

AceFighter19: p. 145; The Advertising Archives: p. 156; The British Library, London: p. 84; © The Trustees of the British Museum, London: pp. 16 top, 18, 55, 59, 79, 97, 99, 106, 109, 110, 112, 123, 158; Brooklyn Museum: p. 100; Jose B. Cabajar: p. 73; John Clarke: p. 69; Chensiyuan: p. 144; Jim Coxon: p. 163; Dreamstime: p. 174 (Jaroslaw Kilian); photo Deutsches Museum: p. 91; Neil Ferguson: p. 28; Freeimages: pp. 133 (Jim Epler), 127 top (Claude Coquilleau), 148 (Stewart Aston), 149 (Geri-Jean Blanchard), 150–51 (Adam Short), 160 (Adrian Lynch); Getty Images: pp. 13 (Dieter Spannknebel), 14 (Peter Adams); © 2009 Google iStockphoto: pp. 39 (meanmachine77), 81 (David Parsons), 88–9 (Jasmina Mihoc), 93 (santirf), 115 (duncan1890), 125 (traveller1116), 147 (Marcus Lindstrom), 152 (Jasmin Awad), 166–7 (Dave Hughes), 170 (HAYKIRDI); Library of Congress, Washington, DC: p. 22; Marama Muru-Lanning: p. 42; Helen Nathan: p. 47; Gabriella Possum Nungurrayi: p. 20; NASA: p. 37; photo © Centre Pompidou, MNAM-CCI, Dist. RMN-Grand Palais/Georges Meguerditchian: p. 11; Royal Collection Trust/© Her Majesty Queen Elizabeth II, 2014: pp. 16 bottom, 23, 50; Veronica Strang: pp. 6, 8, 17, 25, 27, 30, 35, 42, 48, 54, 57, 62, 66, 71, 72, 77, 90, 95, 105, 107, 120, 127 bottom, 129, 136, 137, 138, 139, 153, 159, 168; Victoria and Albert Museum, London: p. 15; Chris Watson: p. 45.

INDEX